# HEAVEN STARTS NOW

*Becoming a Saint
Day by Day*

the**WORD**
among us®
*press*

# HEAVEN STARTS NOW

*Becoming a Saint Day by Day*

FR. JOHN RICCARDO

Published by The Word Among Us Press
7115 Guilford Drive
Frederick, Maryland 21704
www.wau.org

20 19 18 17 16   1 2 3 4 5

ISBN: 978-1-59325-301-1
eISBN: 978-1-59325-489-6

Cover design by Faceout Studios

Made and printed in the United States of America

Library of Congress Control Number: 2016950651

# Contents

# Introduction

Here at Our Lady of Good Counsel, we recently remodeled an area behind the sanctuary. The new construction left an open area with a wall directly across from a twenty-four-hour adoration chapel, and we wondered what to do with it. We decided that we wanted people who were walking out of the chapel to be greeted by the saints. So we asked an artist in Florida to paint images of several saints—Elizabeth Ann Seton, Fulton Sheen, Kateri Tekakwitha, Solanus Casey, Mother Cabrini, and Pierre Toussaint.

Why these saints in particular? First, because they are American and, second, because they are modern. They remind us that sainthood and saintliness are not only for people centuries ago, in faraway places such as Europe or the Middle East or Africa. Sainthood is for us, now.

And that's the point of this book. We are called to become saints. Often people will say, "I'm just trying to figure out God's will for my life." In 1 Thessalonians 4:3, St. Paul wrote, "For this is the will of God, your sanctification." That's God's will for you—to become a saint. That's the plan.

The chapters in this book come from talks I gave at my parish. Those attending had completed the ten-week Alpha course. More than two thousand people at OLGC have now been through the program. Its goal is to make disciples—to help people, maybe for the first time in their lives, truly encounter Jesus and the power of his Holy Spirit.

Alpha had a significant impact on the people who completed the course. Based on the evaluations we received, 52 percent said Alpha had a significant or life-changing impact on them. As a result of going through Alpha, they now say they have a deeper faith or have grown in their faith. Of those, 10 percent said they had a life-changing experience with Jesus. That's phenomenal. And that is precisely the goal of Alpha: to lead people into a deeper relationship with Jesus. In *Evangelii Gaudium* (The Joy of the Gospel), Pope Francis explains why it's important that we hear, first and foremost, that Jesus loves us and wants to have a relationship with us.

> The first proclamation must ring out over and over: "Jesus Christ loves you; he gave his life to save you; and now he is living at your side every day to enlighten, strengthen, and free you." This first proclamation is called "first" not because it exists at the beginning and can then be forgotten or replaced by other more important things. It is first in a qualitative sense because it is the principal proclamation, the one which we must hear again and again in different ways. (164)

That message—the proclamation of the love of God—has to precede everything else, he says. Then all else will follow.

> It is the message capable of responding to the desire for the infinite which abides in every human heart. The centrality of the kerygma calls for stressing those elements which are most needed today: it has to express God's saving love which precedes any moral and religious obligation on our part; it should not impose the truth but appeal to freedom; it should be marked by joy, encouragement, liveliness, and a harmonious balance which will not reduce preaching to a few doctrines which are at

times more philosophical than evangelical. All this demands on the part of the evangelizer certain attitudes which foster openness to the message: approachability, readiness for dialogue, patience, a warmth and welcome which is non-judgmental. (165)

That's what happened during Alpha here at OLGC. Participants sat in small groups and felt free to say anything; there was no judgment. The message we heard over and over again was intended to lead us to an encounter with God who is love. And when we experience that love, we can then ask, "What am I supposed to do with this now?" Here is Pope Francis' answer:

The first proclamation also calls for ongoing formation and maturation. Evangelization aims at a process of growth which entails taking seriously each person and God's plan for his or her life. All of us need to grow in Christ. Evangelization should stimulate a desire for this growth, so that each of us can say wholeheartedly: "It is no longer I who live, but Christ who lives in me" (Galatians 2:20). (160)

Jesus said, "I am the Alpha and the Omega, the first and the last, the beginning and the end" (Revelation 22:13). Alpha is the first letter of the twenty-four-letter Greek alphabet, and Omega is the last letter. We start with the kerygma, the proclamation: God loves you so much that he sent his Son to die for you. Omega is the end point—sainthood. The goal is to grow in Christ, as Pope Francis says, so that we can become saints.

So the goal of this book is to help you grow in Christ. In fact, the title is derived from something I heard from the auxiliary bishop of our archdiocese here in Detroit, Bishop Mike

Byrnes. He said, "We need serious application of the Scripture to our lives right now so that we can begin to live the life of heaven *now*, not just *get* to heaven." That's a great distinction. We want to begin now to live the life of heaven.

In the following chapters, we are going to look seriously at Scripture in seven different areas involving issues that we have to grapple with in some way or another in our lives. We want to learn what the Lord says to us about these topics so that we can grow in Christ and let him mold and form us. Questions for your own reflection or for group discussion are included at the end of each chapter.

In our world today, there is an urgent need for saints, ordinary people who surrender their lives to Jesus and become reflections of his own divine nature here on earth. That's how we start living the life of heaven now. There's no time to lose, so let's begin!

# CHAPTER 1

## *What's Your Plan?*

Here's a question I want you to consider: do you, right now, have a plan, and are you working at it, so that one day you will become a saint? Will someone someday want to make a painting or statue of you because of the way you lived your life? We risk misunderstanding the whole point of life if our goal, our plan, is not sainthood. The nineteenth-century French writer Léon Bloy wrote, "The only real sadness, the only real failure, the only great tragedy in life, is not to become a saint."

Recently I met with a young man who had just been diagnosed with cancer. He made the point of saying to me, "You know, Father, I live by goals. I'm very successful at my work because I always have goals in front of me. Goals drive me." Now he realizes he needs new goals. "I need a goal to get through chemo; I need a goal to get through all the treatment. I need some goals that my wife and I can have in front of us going through this, like going on a vacation, celebrating an anniversary." He's right. And there's nothing quite like cancer to wake you up to the fact that as important as all those other goals are, the only real goal, the only ultimate goal that we need to be focused on, is the Omega, which is sainthood. Sainthood is God's hall of fame, and it's within your reach. The grace is a given. All it takes is our work and our cooperation with it.

Saints respond to the needs that they see in their time. If Elizabeth Ann Seton hadn't responded to the need she saw, maybe we wouldn't have Catholic schools in our country today. If Solanus Casey hadn't responded to the call of God in his life, perhaps tens of thousands of people would never have encountered the incredibly healing power of God and his love.

Centuries ago, there was a Spaniard named Iñigo who was one of thirteen children. He had no desire whatsoever for God and certainly no desire for holiness. Instead, he was obsessed with attaining personal glory. He was a womanizer, an expert dancer, and a very fancy dresser. His knee was blown apart in a battle, and because he didn't like the way it had healed—a bone was sticking out and he wanted the ladies to still be attracted to him—he had it rebroken so that it would heal without the bump. While he was convalescing, he asked for some books to be brought to him to pass the time. The only two books available were one on the life of Christ and the other on the saints, so he read them.

And God broke in—and changed everything. The Lord showed him what real glory looks like, what real nobility, real manhood, and real courage looks like. Iñigo changed his name to Ignatius, after St. Ignatius of Antioch, one of the heroes of the early Church, and founded the Society of Jesus (the Jesuits). In the last five-hundred-plus years, literally hundreds of millions of people have come to encounter Jesus through his Spiritual Exercises.

But he's gone now. So are Solanus Casey, Kateri Tekakwitha, and Elizabeth Ann Seton. They have handed the baton to you and to me. And now it's our turn. It's our turn to fight the good fight; it's our turn to run the race; it's our turn to keep the faith. How do we do that?

There are no shortcuts for the next step. We have to take responsibility for what we're going to do to respond. We have to come up with a plan, if you will, to accomplish the goal.

Here's an analogy. When I meet with engaged couples for marriage prep, I urge them to come up with a plan. That's just common sense, right? Businesses tend to fail if they don't have a plan. The same is true for marriages. So I ask the couples to make a pie chart with all the different dimensions they will experience in their life together, such as finances, prayer, intimacy, sex, in-laws, children, and communication. Then I ask them, "For each of those areas, what does heroic virtue look like?" Then this becomes a set of goals for the couple, something they can use so that their marriage will thrive. They pull it out every couple of months, look at it, and ask themselves, "How are we doing with that?"

So it is with sainthood. We need a business plan for sainthood. Now, that might sound strange. How do you plan sainthood? Well, Pope St. John Paul II says that you can. In a letter he wrote, *Novo Millennio Ineunte* (At the Beginning of the New Millennium), he says this:

Can holiness ever be "planned"? What might the word "holiness" mean in the context of a pastoral plan? . . . To ask catechumens: "Do you wish to receive Baptism?" means at the same time to ask them: "Do you wish to become holy?" It means to set before them the radical nature of the Sermon on the Mount: "Be perfect as your heavenly Father is perfect" (Matthew 5:48). As the Council itself explained, this ideal of perfection must not be misunderstood as if it involved some kind of extraordinary existence, possible only for a few "uncommon heroes" of holiness. The ways of holiness are many, according to the vocation of each individual. . . . The time has come to re-propose wholeheartedly to everyone this *high standard of ordinary Christian living*: the whole life of the Christian community and of Christian families must lead in this direction. (31)

I have to plan to become a saint. So what does that look like? This is something we can't fudge; we have to write down a plan. Here is a series of things to think about. This is not an exhaustive list; it's just a way to get us started:

*Prayer.* What do I consider greatness to look like in prayer? What do I think I need to do every day in terms of prayer to become a saint? Don't ask the question, "Do I pray enough?" The answer is no—no one prays enough; it's not possible. But am I praying as much as I should be praying?

*Scripture.* There is no way I am able to let God form me if I don't read his word. I have to let him form me, and he forms me through the Scriptures.

*Service.* Do I reach out of myself? Do I look to volunteer, whether it is in the parish, the local community, or with the poor?

*Confession.* Do I have as my goal getting to Confession once every two months? If that's not on your list, I'd start there. And if you haven't been to Confession in years, just come back. Just come back!

*Mass.* Obviously, we need to go to Sunday Mass. But ask yourself this: is it possible for me to achieve greatness when I am feeding on the Eucharist only once a week? Once we've really come to understand, objectively speaking, that the Eucharist is the *greatest* source of strength that we could ever encounter in our lives, why wouldn't we want to come more often? Some of us can't go to Mass more than once a week because of work. But maybe we can try to get there once during the week, in addition to Sunday. Many people who start coming during the week end up coming every day as they gradually realize, "I just can't thrive without the Eucharist. I'm not strong enough. I used to think I was, but now I've come to realize otherwise."

*Sin.* What are the one or two really significant obstacles in my life right now that are keeping me from reaching the goal of sainthood? How am I going to overcome those? Am I just going to say to myself, "Well, that's just the way I am"? Or am I going to let the Lord change me?

*Fasting.* Do I ever fast? Jesus doesn't say, "*If* you fast . . . "; he says, "*When* you fast . . . " What is my plan for fasting? Some of us can't fast from food because of health reasons, but we can fast from something else, like the news or the time we spend looking at our computers or cell phones.

*Alms.* Do I give alms? Do I look at the resources that I have as a means by which I can share with the poor? Pope Francis is constantly reminding us of our obligation to do what we can to help the poor. He wants us not just to care for them so that they simply receive our mercy but, instead, to lift them up and set them on their feet and get them on their way. That's what he's encouraging us to do.

My encouragement for you in the weeks ahead is to ask yourself, "Do I have a plan to become a saint?" And if you don't, what is your plan going to look like? Then start working on it. Let's do the work! I think you'll be amazed at how helpful it is.

## QUESTIONS FOR REFLECTION AND DISCUSSION

1. What is the goal of your life? Have you ever thought that your goal should be to become a saint? Why or why not?

2. Who is your favorite saint and why? How might you emulate that saint?

3. Do you have a plan to become a saint? If so, what is it? If not, what might it include?

# Chapter 2

# *Forgiveness*

Why is forgiveness so important? Why are we starting here? Listen to what the preacher to the papal household, Fr. Raniero Cantalamessa, has to say: "Forgiveness does for a community what oil does for a motor. If someone begins a trip in a car without a drop of oil in the engine, after a few minutes the whole car will be on fire. Like oil, forgiveness neutralizes friction."[1]

I would suggest that this is a perfect place to begin, especially as we embark on this trip headed toward the Omega, which is sainthood. If we're going to be serious about becoming saints, then it means we are going to have to tackle this particular issue.

A lack of forgiveness is the single most significant stumbling block we can face in reaching the goal of becoming saints, of living the life of heaven now. I also think forgiveness is the single most difficult thing to do in life. In fact, I would suggest that it's impossible to do. If you've ever had an enemy, you know that. If you've never had an enemy, then you think that Jesus' words in the Sermon on the Mount are beautiful. But the moment that you have an enemy, you think, "Oh, surely, Lord, you didn't mean *that*. You could *not* have meant to forgive *that*." And the Lord says, "Um, yes. Actually, I did."

Remember what the Lord said through St. Paul in 1 Thessalonians 4:3: "For this is the will of God, your sanctification." What does it mean to be sanctified, to be holy, to become a

saint? To be sanctified means that the Lord has taken possession of me. I'm the first person to say that this hasn't entirely
happened to me. But I want it, most days. (Not all days, most
days!) That's the goal—that's the Omega. We start with hearing the proclamation of the gospel and what it is that Jesus
has done for us. That's the Alpha. Now it's about responding. And again, many of us have been responding, some of us
for decades, praise God. But there's always more we can do.

## God's Perspective on Sin

In the previous chapter, we talked about St. Ignatius and his
remarkable encounter with the Lord. As Ignatius reflected on
how God had moved in his life, he put together the Spiritual
Exercises. In their ideal form, the Exercises are done as a month-
long retreat, four weeks of intense immersion into Scripture.
The retreatant spends hours and hours in prayer every day.

But Ignatius begins his Exercises in a unique way. God had
shown him how to teach and lead others to conversion, and
that was to begin by first getting God's own perspective on
sin. So as I begin praying through the Exercises, I am trying
to get an objective perspective on sin. I want to see what God
thinks about it. Only then can I apply that perspective on sin
to myself. If I start to apply it to myself right away, I will either
be crushed, or I will have no capacity to be objective.

So Ignatius begins with a reflection on the sin of the angels,
then on the sin of Adam and Eve, and then on the sin of one
person who might have died in mortal sin, at the end of which
you reach this conclusion: God hates sin. Once you understand
that, then you move into an application to your own life and

you realize, "I don't have just one sin." For one sin, the angels lost paradise. For one sin, Adam and Eve were kicked out of the Garden. For one unrepented sin, someone could forfeit eternal life. But I have *pages* of sin. I have a book, a library of sins. So do you.

And yet I'm still here, and you're still here. And God hasn't just tolerated me. He calls you and me his friends. He invites us to be about the work of spreading the gospel. He calls us, each in our own way, to be ambassadors of the gospel and to be tangible touches of him for other people. That's remarkable.

So first we want to get God's mind on sin and forgiveness. In 1980, Pope St. John Paul II wrote an encyclical on the heavenly Father called *Dives in Misericordia*, meaning "Rich in Mercy." "Rich in mercy" is taken from St. Paul's letter to the Ephesians (2:4)—and that's what God is, rich in mercy. God loves to forgive. Let that sink in: God, the One who is offended by every single sin that is committed, loves to forgive.

We can have a hard time with the idea that God could be offended by our sin. But try to think of it in terms of football. What does it mean to go on the offense? It means to go on the attack. In some way or another, all of our sin is an attack against God—this God who is continually, daily, relentlessly assaulted, who is blasphemed, spurned, ignored, and cursed. This is the God who loves to forgive. As the prophet Micah wrote,

> Who is a God like you, pardoning iniquity
>     and passing over transgression . . . ?
> He does not retain his anger for ever
>     because he delights in mercy. . . .

You will cast all our sins
    into the depths of the sea. (Micah 7:18, 19)

Unfortunately, many of us are not yet convinced that God's mercy applies to us, to whatever is in our past. We think it's for the other people we know who have done minor things wrong in their lives. But God's mercy is for everyone. That is the truth. As you read these words, maybe the evil one, who loves to slander us, is holding up in front of you images of your past, calling you names, doing whatever it is that he does. If so, ask the Holy Spirit to help you know that this is for *you*. Because God wants to heal *you*. He wants to make it abundantly clear that no matter what is in our past, he wants to forgive us.

And we don't have to be perfect right now to ask God for forgiveness. It's not a question of you or me first getting our act together and then being able to present ourselves to the Lord and saying, "How about now? Are you happy with me now? Now that I've done all this?" No, he just wants to wash us clean, now, wherever we find ourselves.

Here are some snippets from my favorite psalm, Psalm 103:

Bless the LORD, O my soul;
    and all that is within me, bless his holy name! . . .
who forgives all your iniquity, . . .
who redeems your life from the Pit. . . .
The LORD is merciful and gracious,
    slow to anger and abounding in mercy. . . .
He does not deal with us according to our sins. (103:1, 3, 4, 8, 10)

So while the evil one is trying to tell us lies, saying, "No, that's not for you," here's how you know this *is* for you: this is the word of God. It's true, and it's speaking to us right now. God does not treat us according to our sins, or we'd all be toast. But you're here and I'm here. How do you know God loves you? You're here—that's how. More from Psalm 103:

> nor [does he] repay us according to our iniquities.
> For as the heavens are high above the earth,
>> so great is his mercy toward those who fear him;
> as far as the east is from the west,
>> so far does he remove our transgressions from us. (103:10-12))

I'd recommend that you copy these passages into a prayer journal so you can go take some time to pray with them. The Holy Spirit—the Spiritual Director—is the one who wants to take us deeper into these truths. He wants us to seriously apply Scripture to our lives. So if these verses are touching you, spend some time in prayer with them. For now, however, let's turn to Jesus' words on God's mercy and forgiveness.

This is from Jesus' parable of the lost sheep: "Just so, I tell you, there will be more joy in heaven over one sinner who repents than over ninety-nine righteous persons who need repentance" (Luke 15:7). Jesus asks, "What man of you, having a hundred sheep, if he has lost one of them, does not leave the ninety-nine in the wilderness, and go after the one which is lost, until he finds it?" (15:4). Well, the answer to that question is that none of you would. No shepherd does that. Sheep are stupid—we know that. You don't leave ninety-nine sheep because they will just disperse. The "smart" shepherd who is concerned with his profits writes off the one sheep that's lost and protects the other ninety-nine. The Good Shepherd says, "I'm going back to get that one." Commenting on this parable, Pope Francis said,

> That is the most profound message of this story: the joy of God, a God who doesn't like to lose. God is not a good loser, and this is why, in order not to lose, he goes out on his own, and he goes, he searches. He is a God who searches: he searches for all those who are far away from him, like the shepherd who goes to search for the lost sheep. . . . He is a God who walks around searching for us, and has a certain loving weakness for those who are furthest away, who are lost.[2]

Whoever it is that is lost, maybe our kids or our grandkids, or whomever we are afraid for, be at peace. God is not a good loser. He's on his way to find them.

Immediately after this parable in Luke 15 is the story of the lost coin. The woman who loses a coin searches the house, finds the coin, and throws a party that costs more than the coin she had lost. Then again Jesus says, "Just so, I tell you, there is joy before the angels of God over one sinner who repents" (15:10). I don't know about you, but I find that hard to believe. I find it easy to believe that this was the case twenty-six years ago when I walked into a confessional. I came back into the sheepfold, so to speak, and I've never been lost since then. And yet I find it impossible, from my human perspective, to understand how God could be rejoicing over the fact that I'm back in the confessional every two weeks and I'm confessing my sins all over again. But he *is!* Don't misunderstand me—he does not delight in our sins. But every single time we confess, he rejoices. Why? Because he doesn't have a memory of what's in the past.

When we walk into a confessional, we might be thinking, "I was just here three weeks ago with the same thing. Surely God is keeping track of all these sins, all these pages and pages of them. And the book is getting long." But God doesn't have that book. "As far as the east is from the west, / so far does he remove our transgressions from us" (Psalm 103:12). He doesn't keep a tally, as we're soon going to see.

Back to Luke 15, and we come upon the greatest story of all of God's richness in mercy, the parable of the prodigal son. After we've come home, our Father says,

> "Bring quickly the best robe, and put it on him; and put a ring on his hand, and shoes on his feet; and bring the fatted calf and kill it, and let us eat and make merry; for this my son was dead, and is alive again; he was lost, and is found." And they began to make merry. (Luke 15:22-24)

St. Faustina wrote about God's mercy, and while it is private revelation and not something we are not obliged to believe, her words are very consistent with Scripture. For example, our Lord said to her, "Let the greatest sinners place their trust in My mercy. They have the right before others to trust in the abyss of My mercy."[3] This is everything that Jesus is doing when he is proclaiming the gospel. People are gawking at his forgiveness of sinners, and he's trying to tell us all, "No, these are the ones who need to know that they can receive God's mercy." And that's what the Lord is saying to us. We may feel as if we do not deserve it, but he is saying to us, "No, no, you're supposed to be receiving my mercy. This is for you."

Here is something else our Lord told St. Faustina:

My daughter, write about My mercy towards tormented souls. Souls that make an appeal to My mercy delight me. To such souls I grant even more graces than they ask. I cannot punish even the greatest sinner if he makes an appeal to My compassion, but on the contrary, I justify him in My unfathomable and inscrutable mercy. Write: before I come as a just Judge, I first open wide the door of My mercy.[4]

God will come as a just judge—make no mistake about that. But he first wants to come as a merciful Lord. We just have to come to him.

## Delight in Showing Mercy

But there is a catch: "Blessed are the merciful, for they shall obtain mercy" (Matthew 5:7). Jesus taught us to pray, "Forgive us our trespasses *as*"—note the word "as"—"we forgive those who trespass against us."

I know of a woman, a mystic who lived in the twentieth century, who was an inspiration to Pope St. John Paul II on a number of matters. For a long time, maybe years, she would not pray the Our Father because of some bitterness she was harboring. She knew that she couldn't pray the Lord's Prayer with integrity. Because when I pray it with integrity, I am telling God to forgive me as I forgive others, most especially that person who is on my mind right now, whom I'm really *afraid*

God wants me to forgive. "For if you forgive men their trespasses, your heavenly Father also will forgive you; but if you do not forgive men their trespasses, neither will your Father forgive your trespasses" (Matthew 6:14-15).

St. Paul wrote, "Put on then, as God's chosen ones, holy and beloved, compassion, kindness, lowliness, meekness, and patience, forbearing one another and, if one has a complaint against another, forgiving each other; as the Lord has forgiven you, so you also must forgive" (Colossians 3:12-13). It is very important to understand: we should have mercy *because* we have been mercifully treated, not so that we'll receive mercy. Does that make sense? It's an important adjustment. It's not as if we say, "Okay, in order for me to *get* forgiven, I have to forgive *you*." Instead, as I come to understand what the Lord has done for me—and here's the kicker!—I have to *delight* in showing mercy. It doesn't mean that I feel delight in my emotions; it means that I want to take on the mind of Christ, who loves to be merciful.

Using some very rich language, the section in the *Catechism of the Catholic Church* on the Lord's Prayer says this:

> This petition is astonishing. If it consisted only of the first phrase, "And forgive us our trespasses," it might have been included, implicitly, in the first three petitions of the Lord's Prayer, since Christ's sacrifice is "that sins may be forgiven." But, according to the second phrase, our petition will not be heard unless we have first met a strict requirement. Our petition looks to the future, but our response must come first, for the two parts are joined by the single word "as." . . .

Now—and this is daunting—this outpouring of mercy cannot penetrate our hearts as long as we have not forgiven those who have trespassed against us. Love, like the Body of Christ, is indivisible; we cannot love the God we cannot see if we do not love the brother or sister we do see (cf. 1 John 4:20). In refusing to forgive our brothers and sisters, our hearts are closed and their hardness makes them impervious to the Father's merciful love; but in confessing our sins, our hearts are opened to his grace.

This petition is so important that it is the only one to which the Lord returns and which he develops explicitly in the Sermon on the Mount (cf. Matthew 6:14-15; 5:23-24; Mark 11:25). This crucial requirement of the covenant mystery is impossible for man. But "with God all things are possible" (Matthew 19:26). (2838, 2840–41)

This is my whole point from the start and what the *Catechism* says below: *it is impossible to keep the Lord's commandment by imitating the divine model from outside.* There has to be a vital participation coming from the depths of the heart. This is sanctification. Sanctification is for me to be possessed by God. And we begin here with this topic precisely because, undoubtedly, many of us are thinking, "I don't know how I'm going to do that." Which is why we have to start here, because unless we do, we're never going to make progress. Continuing with the *Catechism*:

This "as" is not unique in Jesus' teaching: "You, therefore, must be perfect, *as* your heavenly Father is perfect"; "Be merciful, even *as* your Father is merciful"; "A new commandment I give to you, that you love one another, even *as* I have loved you, that you also love one another" (Matthew 5:48; Luke 6:36; John 13:34). It is impossible to keep the Lord's commandment by imitating the divine model from outside; there has to be a vital participation, coming from the depths of the heart, in the holiness and the mercy and the love of our God. Only the Spirit by whom we live can make "ours" the same mind that was in Christ Jesus (cf. Galatians 5:25; Philippians 2:1, 5). Then the unity of forgiveness becomes possible and we find ourselves "forgiving one another, *as* God in Christ forgave" us (Ephesians 4:32). (2842)

I'm going to break this open a little more at the end of the chapter. But let me stress: forgiveness is not a question of trying harder; it's a question of letting the Holy Spirit come more deeply into our lives. We have to acknowledge, "I can't do this. But I'm not on my own. All things are possible for God. And you, Lord, live in me. And you live in me with the intention and the goal of transforming me into the person of Jesus. So here I am, Lord; here's my heart. It's a mess. Do something."

## Stop Counting

Now, after getting the Lord's mind on mercy and forgiveness, I want to turn to what is the most important lesson from Jesus on forgiveness.

Peter comes to Jesus with a question: "How often do I have to forgive my brother?" (cf. Matthew 18:21). Now, it is worth knowing that this was actually a common question that rabbis were asked. One rabbi, a contemporary of Jesus, wrote, "If a man commits an offense, let him be pardoned a first, second, and a third time, but not the fourth." This is the human condition apart from grace. We think, "You know, I've forgiven this person so many times; he's had enough chances."

Jesus' response is, "No, not seven times. You [insert your name], not seven times, but seventy-seven times" (cf. Matthew 18:22). Which means, "Stop counting." Seven is the number that represents fullness; it represents an infinite amount. Stop counting. Stop keeping track. Stop keeping score. That's what we do, isn't it, in our relationships, especially in our marriages? We keep score. Stop keeping score. If I'm serious about living the life of discipleship and growing into conformity with Jesus, I can't do that. I want to do it—I do it a lot—but I can't.

And then Jesus tells a parable. Peter asks a question, and to answer the question, Jesus tells a story. Why? Jesus wants us to feel the impact of the story so that we will understand more profoundly what he has done for us. That's what stories do. Here is the parable he tells:

> "Therefore the kingdom of heaven may be compared to a king who wished to settle accounts with his servants. When he began the reckoning, one was brought to him who owed him ten thousand talents; and as he could not pay, his lord ordered him to be sold, with his wife and children and all that he had, and payment to be made. So the servant fell on his knees, imploring him, 'Lord, have patience with me, and I will pay you everything.' And out of pity for him the lord of that servant released him and forgave him the debt. But that same servant, as he went out, came upon one of his fellow servants who owed him a hundred denarii; and seizing him by the throat he said, 'Pay what you owe.' So his fellow servant

fell down and pleaded with him, 'Have patience with me, and I will pay you.' He refused and went and put him in prison till he should pay the debt. When his fellow servants saw what had taken place, they were greatly distressed, and they went and reported to their lord all that had taken place. Then his lord summoned him and said to him, 'You wicked servant! I forgave you all that debt because you pleaded with me; and should not you have had mercy on your fellow servant, as I had mercy on you?' And in anger his lord delivered him to the jailers, till he should pay all his debt." (Matthew 18:23-34)

Now, be sure to underline Jesus' concluding sentence: *"So also my heavenly Father will do to every one of you, if you do not forgive your brother from your heart"* (Matthew 18:35).

Let's try to understand this in a deeper way. What was the value of ten thousand talents? Ten thousand was the highest number used in counting at the time of Jesus; it is often translated as "myriads." A talent was the largest currency used in the Middle East at the time of Jesus. So this is the highest number as well as the largest currency that was used. To put it in perspective, the tax tribute for an entire district at the time of Jesus would have been about two hundred talents. This man owes ten thousand talents. This is an amount beyond conception.

Let me break it down for you. Ten thousand talents was the equivalent of one hundred million denarii. A denarius was a daily wage. Ten thousand talents is the equivalent of one hundred million days' wages. This man owes 273,972 years' pay. We could have been paying off the Lord every day since his ascension into heaven, and we would still owe him a little more than 271,000 years' pay!

We have been forgiven an amount that is beyond anything we could ever imagine. Maybe we don't have a dramatic conversion story because we were never that far from God, but it doesn't matter. Whether we had a huge conversion or not, you and I, because of the nature of sin as an offense against God, owe him a debt that we could never pay back ourselves.

Maybe we don't think we sin that often. It's an odd paradox that the saints are the people who accuse themselves of being sinful more often than the rest of us. Why is that the case? It's not because they are masochists; it's not because they have some big ego-deficit complex. It's because as they get closer and closer to Jesus, the flaws in their own lives jump out all the more, and they want to change.

In this parable, the first man said to the Lord, "Lord, give me time and I'll repay you" (cf. Matthew 18:26). Good luck with that. You're not going to live 274,000 years. What does the Lord do? The Lord says, "You know what, how about this? Forget the time. Let's just forget it all." And he rips up the promissory note. That isn't even what the man has asked for. But his plea has been answered. Your plea, my plea, has been answered in an unexpected, unhoped-for, unimaginable way. The Lord just says, "Hey, forget it."

But our forgiveness wasn't cheap. Grace isn't cheap. Grace comes with a cost. The cost of that note being ripped up was the blood of Jesus.

God could have forgiven me just by saying, "I forgive you," but he didn't. He could have forgiven the whole world that way, but he didn't. He could have forgiven the whole world by the shedding of just one drop of Jesus' blood, but he didn't. His body was, almost literally, wrung out. By the time he had expired on the cross, there was no fluid left in Jesus' body. That was the cost.

In comparison, what does someone else owe me? This is not to say that what we've done to each other or what has been done to us is trivial. That's not the point. I've had horrific things happen to me in my life. Many of us have. But in comparison to what God has done for me—forgiven me—nothing anyone has done can compare. It's the equivalent of someone owing me three months' worth of wages, which is what the second servant in the parable owed the first man.

This is what the *Catechism* has to say about this parable:

> The parable of the merciless servant . . . ends with these words: "So also my heavenly Father will do to every one of you, if you do not forgive your brother from your heart" (cf. Matthew 18:23-35). It is there, in fact, "in the depths of the heart," that everything is bound and loosed. *It is not in our power* not to feel or to forget an offense; but the heart that offers itself to the Holy Spirit turns injury into compassion and purifies the memory in transforming the hurt into intercession." (2843, emphasis added)

Every time I remember the people who have wronged me, I have a choice. I can pray for them and forgive them, or I can become bitter and angry and resentful all over again. It's my choice, and it's the same with all of us.

Do you struggle in your prayer life right now? Have you been unable to make any progress? This might be one of the reasons; maybe you have some resentment you need to deal with. That is what the *Catechism* is reminding us of:

Christian prayer extends to the *forgiveness of enemies*, transfiguring the disciple by configuring him to his Master. Forgiveness is a high-point of Christian prayer; only hearts attuned to God's compassion can receive the gift of prayer. Forgiveness also bears witness that, in our world, love is stronger than sin. The martyrs of yesterday and today bear this witness to Jesus. Forgiveness is the fundamental condition of the reconciliation of the children of God with their Father and of men with one another. (2844)

And then there is this exhortation from St. Cyprian, who is quoted in the *Catechism*, which is really worth our keeping in mind when we come forward for Communion and when we exchange the sign of peace. It's rather direct.

God does not accept the sacrifice of a sower of disunion, but commands that he depart from the altar so that he may first be reconciled with his brother. For God can be appeased only by prayers that make peace. To God, the better offering is peace, brotherly concord, and a people made one in the unity of the Father, Son, and Holy Spirit. (2845)

This is serious stuff for a Christian community or a parish. We cannot be sowing disunity. What does the Lord say to us in the Sermon on the Mount? "Depart and get right with me, make peace with your brother and sister, and, when you've done that, then you come back to the altar. Do not give me this pious façade of thinking that all is well" (cf. Matthew 5:23-25).

Fr. Cantalamessa, whom we quoted at the beginning of this chapter, also said this: "Being merciful appears . . . as an essential aspect to being 'in the image and likeness of God.'"[5]

If I really want to be a saint, mercy is one of those essential qualities that I need to have. That's why we begin here. The house is only going to be as strong as the foundation, and this is the foundation of the house. How does forgiveness happen? How am I able to forgive? It doesn't happen by trying harder. It doesn't happen by rolling up our sleeves and saying, "Ah, I just have to get on with the work of forgiving, then." No, it happens by grace.

God is already working in you and me through faith. He's working right now, and he's saying, "You know, it's time. It's time to let it go, to forgive, to give me your heart, to let me soften it. It's time. Now! It's time."

God's work is happening within us. It happens by the Holy Spirit helping me to understand that the cross of Jesus was, and *is*, for me. The block for many of us is simply this: we don't realize what the Lord has done for us, how he has forgiven us. To help us understand, we can go to the Lord. We can implore him by praying this prayer this week:

*Holy Spirit, you live in me. I need you to help me know, like I've never known before, that your death on the cross was for me. Help me to know what you have forgiven me for. Help me to know what I deserve, even though you don't treat me as my sins deserve. Help me to know that you have rescued my life from destruction.*

And when we do gain some insight, we can ask ourselves: what does someone do who has had his or her whole debt ripped up? How can I hold on to *anything* after what I've been forgiven?

Here are some questions you can reflect on or discuss in a small-group setting. Invite the Holy Spirit to be present, and see what light the Lord sheds on you. Then let it change your life.

## QUESTIONS FOR REFLECTION AND DISCUSSION

1. What does forgiveness *not* mean? (It doesn't mean we have to forget. God does that; you and I don't.)

2. What *does* forgiveness mean? What does it *really* mean to forgive someone?

3. What is the key to forgiveness?

4. How have you experienced forgiveness transforming your life?

# CHAPTER 3

## *Fear and Anxiety*

In St. Paul's second letter to his good friend Timothy, he wrote, "All Scripture is inspired by God and profitable for teaching, for reproof, for correction, and for training in righteousness" (3:16). One of the ways in which the expression "for teaching, for reproof, for correction" can be understood is that Scripture is helpful for taking something that is bent in us and making it straight.

So, for example, going back to our last chapter on forgiveness, some of us at times have a "bent" understanding of what it means to forgive. We might think, "I'll forgive someone who has hurt me a little, but not someone who has really, really wronged me." Scripture is trying to straighten us up and say, "No, you have to forgive the big and the little."

Our goal, then, is twofold. First, we want to do a quick survey of Scripture so that we can "soak" in the word of God, to get his mind on the topic. And second, we want to apply the word of God to our lives so that we can begin to live the life of heaven *now*. Not just so that we can learn how to *get* to heaven—those are two really different things. And the more we begin to live the life of heaven now, the more we grow in holiness and the happier we become. Remember, God wants us to be saints: "For this is the will of God, your sanctification" (1 Thessalonians 4:3).

In this chapter, I want to look at the word of God regarding fear and anxiety. I am hoping that God will take what's bent in us and straighten it. So if you are either anxious or fearful about something, here is an opportunity to soak in God's word. He is saying to us, "Why don't you just submerge yourself in Scripture? Just rest in my truth, and let me remind you of the reasons why you should not let fear overwhelm you."

If our failure to forgive is the biggest hurdle to our sanctification—his taking possession of me—then perhaps the second biggest hurdle is fear and anxiety. It cripples many of us.

Perhaps you've heard that the command to not be afraid is said more often than anything else in the Bible. That is something I always find a bit disturbing, frankly. If this is what God has to say more than anything else, that means that more than anything else, this is what is happening to us—we're becoming afraid! So it's encouraging on the one hand, but it's sobering on the other.

As we start thinking about this topic, let's begin with a passage that has always struck me. This is what God says through the prophet Isaiah: "Do not fear what they fear, nor be in dread" (8:12).

Who are "they"? "They" are the pagans. God is speaking to the people of Israel, and "they" are those who don't know him. What do they fear? Everything! You name it, they fear it—the loss of money, the loss of health, the loss of the people they love.

Why do they fear? Because they don't know God. And one of the things for us to think about is this: are we any different? Don't misunderstand me—I'm not asking if we are better or worse than the pagans or any nonbeliever. But as believers, there should be something striking about us. One of the things that people should see in us, one of the most striking things, is that while the world around us is riddled with fear, we are not. We have the same occasions for fear as they do, but somehow believers should not be overwhelmed by fear. Don't misunderstand the command "Don't be afraid" as meaning "Don't have the emotion of fear." That would be impossible, and that's not what it means. It means, "Don't be overwhelmed by whatever it is that is threatening to make you afraid."

Those who don't know God have no other options. But those of us who do know God should be significantly and attractively different. We should not be gripped by fear.

## Contrasting Worldviews

Let me take the opportunity now to contrast the pagan worldview of the ancient world with the Christian worldview, because it has something to do with how we think about fear and anxiety.

The pagans believed that there were many gods. The cosmic understanding of the Mesopotamians, the Greeks, the Romans, or any people in the ancient world was that there existed above them a whole host of gods who were basically projections of human beings. They got angry, they stole, they were lustful, they killed, and they were capricious. And these gods were not even in charge. They were subject to the fates of other gods who were above them and controlled them. In turn, all the gods controlled the fates of the human beings whom they had created.

Some scholars teach that Genesis is just like other ancient Near Eastern creation stories. But it's not, and that's because of the difference in its worldview. In the ancient worldview, the gods created humans but not for any grandiose purpose. Genesis tells us that God made men and women in his image and likeness, which is totally different from any of the ancient Near Eastern understandings. Just as important, God created us not to be slaves but for friendship. So God created us out of love, and he made us with a purpose and with a point, a goal in mind, a destiny. We come to understand our destiny through what Jesus has revealed to us: to partake in God's own divine life forever. The goal of life, if you will, is expressed in 2 Peter 1:4: God made us to partake of the divine nature.

You were made to be *divinized*. I was made to be *divinized*. Not to dissolve into the blob that is God, but for me, as I am, and for you, as you are, to partake of God's own life. That's the end for which we were made. That is not the pagan worldview.

Here is the god in one of those ancient Near Eastern myths, the *Enuma Elish*, talking about the creation of the first man, who is called "Lullu": "Yes, I will create Lullu. Upon him shall be the services of the gods imposed, that they may be at rest." That is *not* Genesis; there is no dignity here. One historian who studied the Sumerians said that they

were firmly convinced that man was fashioned of clay and created for one purpose only: to serve the gods by supplying them with food, drink, and shelter so that they might have full leisure for their divine activities. Man's life was beset with uncertainty and haunted by insecurity, since he did not know beforehand the destiny decreed him by the unpredictable gods. When he died, his emasculated spirit descended to the dark, dreary nether world where life was but a dismal and wretched reflection of its earthly counterpart.[6]

What do you get in a worldview like that? You get despair! You conclude, "I'm going to live to maximize pleasure and minimize pain." In that kind of worldview, what could life be about except money, power, and pleasure? There's no point in living otherwise.

Sound familiar? That's our contemporary worldview, a Darwinian evolutionary worldview that says we have evolved from the slime and we're going nowhere. Our being here is just random chance. There is no destiny, no point, no purpose, and no ultimate dignity for you and me. In a worldview like that, fear is rampant.

In the Christian worldview in which God has revealed himself to us—and we wouldn't know this unless God had revealed it—there is one God, not many, and he is good. In fact, he is very good. And everything he made, he has made out of love. We human beings are the pinnacle of his creation because we are made in his image and likeness. Furthermore, he didn't make us to be slaves; he made us for friendship: friendship with him and friendship with one another. And now everything we do fits into a purposeful life, and that changes everything.

## "Fear Not, I Have Redeemed You"

So God says to us, "Fear not." Why? "Because I have redeemed you," meaning, "I have paid a price for you." That's what it means to be redeemed. When we think of the word "redeem," we often think of coupons. But of course, Scripture uses this word over and over again. What the Lord is saying to us in the Old Testament, which is fulfilled in the person of Jesus, is that you and I have been bought—paid for—by him. "Fear not, for I have redeemed you; / I have called you by name" (Isaiah 43:1).

So if we are dealing with fear and anxiety, let this soak in, because this is what God is saying to us: "You are mine." Don't misunderstand me—we are not his possession that he can do whatever he wants with; instead, he is speaking as a bride to her bridegroom or a bridegroom to his bride. God says to each one of us, "I love you more than you could possibly imagine. And I've created everything. Everything I've done, I've done for you. The world I made, I made for you. I made you with a purpose in mind. Don't panic. Understand that when I said I redeemed you, I said it not just with words but with actions— the pouring out of my blood. It was for you because you were worth the trouble." If you know that truth, then all of a sudden the fear begins to dissipate.

Listen to what the Lord says earlier in Isaiah. Remember, he is not just speaking twenty-five hundred years ago but right now to you: "Say to the fearful of heart: / Be strong, do not fear! / Here is your God, / . . . he comes to save you" (Isaiah 35:4, NABRE). That's how much you mean to him; that's how much *we* mean to him. God himself is coming. He's not just going to send an angel. He's not just going to send a prophet. *He* comes to save us.

If you are feeling anxious and fearful as you read this, I hope that the knot in the back of your neck is beginning to relax and that your shoulders are beginning to drop. This is what Scripture is supposed to do; it is supposed to heal us. As we read God's word, this is what we can be thinking: "I'm not alone. I don't have to look out for number one. I have a Father. He loves me. He is good and powerful, and he's always thinking about me; I'm always on his mind. *He comes to save me.*"

Again in Isaiah, the Lord says, "Fear not, for I am with you" (41:10). That's meant for us, right now. No matter what's currently going on in your life—financial concerns, health concerns, concerns about your kids, wondering how in the world you are going to get through whatever transition is in front of you—this is what the Lord says: "Fear not, I am with you. *I am* with you." This God is with you, the master of the universe, the One who never gets nervous, the One who has no rivals.

And continuing on with that verse from Isaiah (41:10), God says, "Be not dismayed, for I am *your* God" (emphasis added). And because he is our God and we belong to him ("You are mine"), then together we can handle whatever is going on in our lives right now.

And so, as we come to hear the Lord speak to us and to know these truths, we can say to him certain things, also from Scripture. Although Psalm 23 is so well known to us, there's a stark admission in it: "Though I walk through the valley of the shadow of death" (verse 4). Maybe we're immersed in grief right now. Maybe we've lost a spouse, a child, a parent, or a sibling in the last few months. We're in the valley of death, and it's not romantic. But though we're there, what does the psalmist say? "I fear no evil." Not because I'm not in the valley of the shadow of death, but because *you*, Lord, are with me. And I know that. And I know who you are. And I know what you've done for me. And I know that you care.

Psalm 27 says something similar: "The Lord is my light and my salvation; / whom shall I fear?" (verse 1). If God is never afraid, never nervous, never scared of anything, and he's on my side, then why should I be afraid? He is with me always, all the time. I just need to learn to turn to him, and I don't always do that.

## Jesus Came to Save Us

We could look at many other passages in the Old Testament. But when we look at the New Testament, the Lord's words take on a different kind of force because of the person of Jesus and the reality of the Incarnation. Remember the passage in Luke in which the angels appear to the shepherds after the birth of Jesus?

> And in that region there were shepherds out in the field, keeping watch over their flock by night. And an angel of the Lord appeared to them, and the glory of the Lord shone around them, and they were filled with fear. (2:8-9)

This is the response to an angel. Angels aren't little cute cherubs! When angels show up in Scripture, they terrify people. The shepherds are filled with fear.

> And the angel said to them, "Be not afraid; for behold, I bring you [us] good news of a *great* joy which will come to all the people; for to you [to us] is born this day in the city of David a Savior, who is Christ the Lord." (Luke 2:10-11, emphasis added)

That's why he has come—he has come to save. In the Old Testament, God said he would come to save us. But it was unthinkable for the Jewish people to try to comprehend that God would actually come to do it in the flesh. But that's what he's done. He didn't send an angel. He didn't commission another Moses. *He* came, and he came to save us.

In the Sermon on the Mount, Jesus talks to us about worry. Listen to the Lord, and remember that this is directly addressed to you and me. This is a passage to take into prayer:

"Do not be anxious about your life, what you shall eat or what you shall drink, nor about your body, what you shall put on. Is not life more than food, and the body more than clothing? Look at the birds of the air: they neither sow nor reap nor gather into barns, and yet your heavenly Father feeds them. Are you not of more value than they? And which of you by being anxious can add one cubit to his span of life? And why are you anxious about clothing? Consider the lilies of the field, how they grow; they neither toil nor spin; yet I tell you, even Solomon in all his glory was not arrayed like one of these. But if God so clothes the grass of the field, which today is alive and tomorrow is thrown into the oven, will he not much more clothe you, O you of little faith? Therefore do not be anxious, saying, 'What shall we eat?' or 'What shall we drink?' or 'What shall we wear?' For the Gentiles seek all these things; and your heavenly Father knows that you need them all. But seek first his kingdom and his righteousness, and all these things shall be yours as well." (Matthew 6:25-33)

What are we anxious about? "Am I ever going to get a job?" or "Am I going to get into the college I want to attend?" or "Is this medical test going to turn out the way I am hoping?'" Jesus says the Gentiles seek these things, but they don't know they have a God, let alone a Father who is good and loving, who made us not to be slaves but to be friends.

Here is a passage we hear at Mass when we come together: "Peace I leave with you; my peace I give to you; not as the world gives do I give to you. Let not your hearts be troubled, neither let them be afraid" (John 14:27). The world gives peace by eliminating conflict. That's the only way the world knows peace. That will never happen in our lives, if for no other reason than that the deepest conflict is the one in our hearts. And that conflict will be raging until the Lord finally finishes purifying us and we are ushered into heaven.

But Jesus gives peace in the midst of conflict, as we're going to see.

## The Storm at Sea

Here's another passage I encourage you take into prayer, especially if you feel as if the Lord is asleep right now:

And when he [Jesus] got into the boat, his disciples followed him. And behold, there arose a great storm on the sea, so that the boat was being swamped by the waves; but he was asleep. And they went and woke him, saying, "Save us, Lord; we are perishing." And he said to them, "Why are you afraid, O men of little faith?" Then he rose and rebuked the winds and the sea; and there was a great calm. And the men marveled, saying, "What sort of man is this, that even winds and sea obey him?" (Matthew 8:23-27)

This image of traveling at sea was a common one in antiquity. And this is what we are doing—we are traveling across the sea that is life. We are heading somewhere, toward a destination. As Christians, we are pilgrims and exiles gathered around the altar, to be nourished by the bread that is so much more than bread; it is the food for the journey to get home. And in our travels across this sea, we discover that this sea often gets violent, just as it was for those disciples who were traveling on a lake.

Don't miss the fact that the apostles are in a storm for one reason—they are following Jesus. If they had not been following Jesus, if they had not been with him, they would not have gotten into the boat. They would have stayed on dry land, and they would have been "safe." But they are following Jesus, and because they are following Jesus, he takes them into a storm. And as he did with them, so often he does with us.

Jesus takes us into storms for many reasons. One of them is to remind us that we are dreadfully in need. Maybe we're feeling pretty secure right now. Maybe we have saved up some money, maybe our health is fairly good, maybe our kids are doing well.

But then we come back from the doctor with a diagnosis that we didn't want to hear, and all of a sudden, we panic. Yet in reality, nothing has changed. We were in God's hands before, when everything was going well (or so we thought), and we're in God's hands now. The God who was with us when we thought we were doing just fine and when we really didn't need him all that much is the same God who is still with us. But now we're painfully reminded, "Oh my, I'm in desperate need."

And if you've never been in such a storm, as a Baptist preacher I admire says, "Keep on living, because God will take you there." God will take us there out of love, to destroy the illusion that we are independent, because we are anything but independent.

So Jesus leads us into the storm. To follow the Lord is not to be protected; this is not magic. This is why it's so important to know Scripture. Oftentimes, when people are in a crisis, when the storms come and they think they shouldn't have come, they say, "I'm trying to live a good life. I'm trying to do all that Jesus has asked me to do, so how could this happen?" We think that way because we don't read the word of God, because we think that somewhere God has promised us something that he never really promised us. We think that if we just follow him, nothing bad will ever happen to us. He said no such thing. In fact, he told us that if we follow him, it could be potentially disastrous. Remember that passage? "Deny yourself, take up your cross, and follow me" (cf. Matthew 16:24; Mark 8:34; Luke 9:23). This is not a picnic! So he leads us into the storm.

Here are some other observations about this passage. First, it's not just any storm. The Greek word used is *seismos*. Do you know what a seismograph measures? Earthquakes. This is an indescribably violent storm; everything is shaking. Knowing that helps us apply the passage to all the different situations that we might be going through right now in our lives, whether it's with our work, our health, our family, the death of a friend, or a crisis of faith. As one commentator puts it, "Matthew wants us to experience the naked fear of an insecurity that has no name, only an impending sense of dread."

Second, the boat isn't just swamped; it's covered—"baptized," if you will. It's being drenched, which creates the feeling of drowning. Perhaps that's how we feel if we're in the middle of a storm right now. Jesus leads the apostles into the storm, and then he seems to withdraw. Jesus is in the boat as all this is happening, and he is sleeping. Notice what is being revealed here: the fact that Jesus is with the disciples, or with us, doesn't keep the storm from coming. In fact, he seems to act like a lightning rod; he attracts the storms.

Jesus is also getting soaked. In the painting by Rembrandt called *Christ in the Storm on the Lake of Galilee*, he is at the bottom of the boat. Erasmo Leiva-Merikakis, in a commentary on the Gospel of Matthew, says this:

> Jesus allows the situation to become hopeless. All human effort and wisdom have been exhausted, and even then he doesn't volunteer an intervention. The disciples have left the near shore physically, and now they must leave human certitudes behind, psychologically and spiritually. They must enter a terrible zone of bottomless distress where nothing stable can be clung to. Human know-how shrinks miserably in the face of the superior power of nature unleashed, and divine help seems remote, indifferent, for Jesus sleeps. Not only has he led them into danger; once having done it, he seems to withdraw. . . . Does this icon of Jesus asleep in the midst of the storm with the distraught disciples not dramatize the leap from hopeless fear to tested faith?

That's what we're trying to understand: that the Lord allows these things to happen in our lives so that our faith can be tested and get stronger. Then we realize that our faith is not in our own power or in what we thought God would protect us from; it becomes much deeper than that.

In each case [hopeless fear or tested faith], the circumstances are identical: same insecurity, same helplessness, same danger, same solitude, same mortal fear. . . . The only difference is the *presence of Jesus*, which because of his inactivity could pass wholly unperceived. Faith does not magically create a world of harmony where wishes suddenly come true. Faith does not show illness, perils, hatred, and violence to have been mere illusion. In a sense, faith makes the believer even more keenly aware of the pain these things inflict on body and soul; for, if God is God and if Jesus is here present, how can he let the horrors continue? Faith makes us aware of God's 'absent presence' by the very force of the trials faith's self-surrender brings on. The disciples would not be weathering this storm if they hadn't followed Jesus. And yet he sleeps.[7]

Don't we ask that same question all the time: "Lord, where are you? How can you let this happen?" We say, "Lord, we are perishing. Save us." Now remember, this is in the middle of a storm. If you are speaking to someone in the middle of a storm, saying softly, "Please save us. We are perishing," he will never hear you. So you have to scream it. And this is the comical exchange. Imagine that you are in the boat, or just imagine that you are in the situation you are in right now if you are dealing with fear and anxiety. You really feel as if you are drowning. Here is how you have to say it: "LORD, SAVE US." To which Jesus has to answer, yelling back something like this. "WHAT'S THE PROBLEM?"

So what's our reaction? "Huh? What do you mean, 'What's the problem?' WE ARE GOING DOWN!" That's the exchange; that's what Jesus is saying back to us right now in the middle of the storm we're in. "What are you worried about?" And we reply, "What do you mean, 'What are you worried about?' Hello! We're bailing water here. We're drowning. We're going to die!"

And then Jesus rebukes the disciples. What does he say? In the middle of the storm, as they hear the claps of thunder and see the bolts of lightning, as the waves drown the boat and as the winds blow, Jesus looks at them and says, "You cowards. Why are you afraid?"

Why the rebuke? This is important not to get wrong. It's not that they don't have faith; that's why they have awakened him. Clearly, they have faith. They woke him up because they thought he could do something. And he can. But the rebuke is deeper than that. The Lord is saying to them, "You don't think that there could be any kind of peace except the peace that comes from me calming the storm right now. You don't know that it is enough for me to be in the boat with you—even if I don't calm the storm. Even if the thunder keeps coming. Even if the boat keeps getting swamped. Even if the lightning keeps lighting up the sky. You don't know who I am."

Jesus says, "The only peace you know is the peace that comes from no conflict. My peace is infinitely better than that. My peace comes in the middle of disasters. I might calm the storm; I might not. Regardless, be at peace."

For me, St. Maximilian Kolbe has always been the icon of the peace that God gives. Kolbe is the Franciscan priest who was arrested and taken to Auschwitz, who gave up his life for an inmate who survived the war and actually lived to see Kolbe canonized in St. Peter's Square four decades later. Kolbe was in the middle of a starvation bunker in the ground in a concentration camp, being dehydrated to death. And while he was in the middle of this starvation bunker in Auschwitz, a place that perhaps, more than any other, could be equated with hell on earth, Kolbe was singing hymns. He was leading the other nine inmates who were in there dying with him in singing songs. He was under no illusion. He was not thinking, "Ah, one more song and the Lord is just magically going to ride in and take me out of here." He was under no illusion whatsoever. In fact, the Nazis were so ticked off at him that they walked into the cell and injected him with acid to kill him. Because the last thing they wanted happening in Auschwitz was the singing of hymns. That is the peace that only God can give.

And here is why I hate the martyrs. (I love the martyrs, but here's why I hate them.) They show me what I'm capable of. I want to kick and scream and balk and complain, and the martyrs show me there is another way. The martyrs remind us that if we would just have faith the size of a mustard seed, then no matter what it is that is taking place in our lives, we will be at peace. Why? Because we belong to God. And because our lives are in his hands. And because he is never afraid, and he can handle any situation that we could ever face.

## QUESTIONS FOR REFLECTION AND DISCUSSION

1. With regard to fear and anxiety, how am I different from those who have no faith? Do I know that I have a loving Father? How might my peacefulness in a difficult situation provide a witness to those who don't know Christ?

2. Do I mistakenly think that Jesus is going to save me from all storms? Why or why not?

3. When storms do come, what is the first thing I do? What is my first reaction? What should it be?

4. If I am experiencing fear and anxiety in my life right now, what can move me from that fear to confidence in the Lord? Who has been a witness to me who could share with me how they were able to do this? What might I be able to share with others in this regard?

5. If you have the opportunity, ask for someone to pray with you about restoring peace in your life.

# CHAPTER 4

# Suffering

So far we have looked at two significant obstacles to this path to sainthood that God has made us for: unforgiveness and fear. Now I want to address suffering. In some ways, this topic might be even more significant than forgiveness because of the challenges that we experience when suffering comes our way.

Remember: we want to become saints so that we can begin to live the life of heaven now. We want the Lord to take possession of us and of whatever he is doing in our lives. And for this to happen, we need to immerse ourselves in the word of God. Imagine God's word as a pool of water. We want to dive in and surround ourselves with the word of God so that it begins to permeate us.

I want to make it clear that when we talk about suffering, we mean more than just illness. It includes not only physical but also moral pain, which is something that is experienced inside of us on a deeper level than physical pain. Many of us know from our own experience or from caring for others that the body actually reaches something of a threshold with physical pain. Physical pain is endurable; what is not endurable is the torment that comes from feeling as if there's simply no point to the pain.

In his letter on suffering, *Salvifici Doloris* (On the Christian Meaning of Human Suffering), Pope St. John Paul II observed that the Old Testament is, in many ways, a book about suffering. We get a glimpse into so many different kinds of suffering. He lists some of them: the danger of death, the death of loved ones, the lack of children, nostalgia for our homeland, loneliness and abandonment, the unfaithfulness of friends, and moral suffering such as remorse of conscience or the difficulty of understanding why the wicked prosper and the just suffer. "Man suffers," he writes, "whenever he experiences any kind of evil" (7).

Pope Benedict, in his encyclical on hope, *Spe Salvi* (Saved in Hope), talks about the need for us to have witnesses in our lives, "martyrs" in the most generic sense of that word (39). I want to share with you the reflections of someone who is a witness, a martyr, in my life—my mom. I want to share the story of her miraculous healing but, more important, the story of the "undoing," if you will, of the miraculous healing and how it is that my mom lives her life right now.

As I thought about the topic of suffering, I felt led in prayer to call her on the phone. "Mom," I said, "you are the person who has suffered more than anyone else I know, and you have gone through it heroically. What would you want to communicate with regard to this topic? What are the Scripture passages you hold dear, that have given you strength, and what would you want us to take away from listening to you?" In this chapter, I want to share with you what she told me.

First, however, are some Scripture passages that strike me when I think about suffering. My all-time favorite in the Bible is from chapter 2 of Sirach, which begins like this: "My child, when you come to serve the Lord, / prepare yourself for trials. / . . . For in fire gold is tested, / and the chosen, in the crucible of humiliation" (2:1, 5, NABRE).

When I reflected on this passage, I was reminded of a sermon by St. Augustine on the prophet Ezekiel's rebuke of the shepherds of Israel (chapter 34):

> The negligent shepherd fails to say to the believer: My son, come to the service of God, stand fast in fear and in righteousness, and prepare your soul for temptation. A shepherd who does say this strengthens the one who is weak and makes him strong. Such a believer will then not hope for the prosperity of this world. For if he has been taught to hope for worldly gain, he will be corrupted by prosperity. When adversity comes, he will be wounded or perhaps destroyed.
>
> The builder who builds in such manner is not building the believer on a rock but upon sand. But the rock was Christ. . . . What sort of shepherds are they who for fear of giving offense not only fail to prepare the sheep for the temptations that threaten, but even promise them worldly happiness? God himself made no such promise to this world. On the contrary, God foretold hardship upon hardship in this world until the end of time. And you want the Christian to be exempt from these troubles? Precisely because he is a Christian, he is destined to suffer more in this world. . . .
>
> Lift him up from the sand and put him on the rock. Let him be in Christ, if you wish him to be a Christian. Let him turn his thoughts to sufferings, however unworthy they may be in comparison to Christ's. Let him center his attention on Christ, who was without sin, and yet made restitution for what he had not done. Let him consider Scripture, which says to him: He chastises every son whom he acknowledged. Let him prepare to be chastised, or else not seek to be acknowledged as a son.[8]

So many of us, when suffering comes our way, immediately think that God has abandoned us. We think we've done something wrong. And that's just not the case. That's why this is an important topic to address in the context of trying to become saints.

We often hear chapter 3 of the Book of Wisdom proclaimed at funerals. Speaking of those who have died, the author says, "Having been disciplined a little, they will receive great good, / because God tested them and found them worthy of himself; / like gold in the furnace he tried them" (3:5-6).

What does it mean for gold to be refined in fire? Here's a great image from something that appeared in a Christian devotional. A goldsmith was asked, "How do you know when gold is purified? How do you know when it is time to take it out of the fire?" And this was his answer: "The gold is purified when you take the gold out of the fire and look at it, and all you see is your face." That's the image that Scripture is using. God wants to be able to look at each of us and see only the face of his Son. But like gold before it's purified, we contain lots of little impurities, impediments, and other things that have to be burned up. Suffering is how that usually happens.

In 2 Corinthians 4:16-17, St. Paul says, "So we do not lose heart. Though our outer man is wasting away, our inner man is being renewed every day. For this slight momentary affliction is preparing for us an eternal weight of glory beyond all comparison." Of course, that "slight momentary affliction" may last for decades. From the human perspective, that hardly looks like a "slight" or "momentary" affliction. But Scripture reminds us that in the scheme of eternity, it is momentary;

even the whole time we are on earth is in a sense "momentary" compared to eternity.

Commenting on this passage, C. S. Lewis wrote that although we seem ordinary to one another, we "live in a society of possible gods and goddesses," and the person we are talking to today "may one day be a creature which, if you saw it now, you would be strongly tempted to worship."[9] Remember, God made you to be divinized, so if I were to see you as you will look in heaven, I'd be tempted to think that you might be God. That's the eternal weight of glory.

The classical text on suffering is Colossians 1:24. If there is a more difficult passage in the Bible to understand, I'm not sure what it is. St. Paul writes, "I rejoice in my sufferings for your sake, and in my flesh I complete what is lacking in Christ's afflictions for the sake of his body, that is, the Church." Paul rejoices in his suffering! This is a man who has been beaten by rods, scourged several times, stoned and left for dead, and shipwrecked, adrift at sea. How does his suffering fill up what is lacking in the sufferings of Christ? And what could be lacking in Christ's sufferings? We'll get back to that.

Here is one last passage, this one from 1 Peter 4:12-13: "Beloved, do not be surprised at the fiery ordeal which comes upon you to prove you, as though something strange were happening to you. But rejoice in so far as you share Christ's sufferings, that you may also rejoice and be glad when his glory is revealed."

And now on to my mom's story.

## A Miraculous Healing

My mother was born in 1929, and I'm the youngest of her five children. If I could use one word to describe my mom, that word would be "class." Or maybe "elegance." She is the classiest, most elegant woman I have ever known. Born and raised in Grosse Point, Michigan, she is a true white Anglo-Saxon Protestant. Her folks were Methodist, and she attended the Metropolitan Methodist Church in Detroit, not far from the Cathedral of the Blessed Sacrament. Her decision to marry my dad, who was dirt-poor and a Catholic immigrant, didn't go over too well with her family. In fact, my grandmother tried to talk her out of it by saying, "If you marry this man, you will never own a car in your life." Which is ironic, since my dad went on to become a fairly high-ranking executive in an auto company!

A few years before I was born, my mom suffered a debilitating back injury. After I was conceived, her doctors told her that they didn't think she would be able to carry me to term. They gave her several alternatives, and I am grateful that she chose life. Somehow my mom was able to carry me and give birth. Until I was about twelve or thirteen years old, my mom was seriously disabled. She lived in a hospital bed in our living room. She wore a special brace around her back all the time. She had special chairs to sit in. She couldn't sit or stand for a long time. She couldn't walk. She was in many ways an invalid. She had a whole host of surgeries on her back, going back and forth to a hospital in New York that specialized in such care.

Then my oldest sister graduated from college and moved away. She was living in another city and went to some kind of

Pentecostal or charismatic prayer meeting. And while she was there, someone had a strong sense that God wanted to heal a person with a serious back injury who wasn't even in the room. And so my sister got very excited and called my mom and said, "Mom, I just came from this meeting. There was this person there with this sense—I think it's you!" My mom said to her, "Honey, I wish I had your faith." My mom was a devout woman, but I think she would tell you that she really didn't know Jesus at the time. But she was about to meet him in a really powerful way.

Mom hung up the phone and said to herself, "What do I have to lose?" So she started to thank God for healing her. Within a month, my mom was playing tennis! Out with the braces, out with the chairs, out with the hospital bed. We built a tennis court in our backyard. My mom joined a tennis club and became the club champion. All of a sudden, she was the most athletic person I had ever seen in my life! It was right out of the Gospels, right out of the Acts of the Apostles; it was a New Testament miracle extraordinaire.

Because of her disability, for years my dad had been going to company meetings and events without her. Then he started bringing her along. People would come up to her and say, "Oh hi, who are you?" "I'm Thelma Riccardo." "Oh, I've never seen you before." "Oh, that's because Jesus just healed my back."

Talk about a conversation stopper! But that's what happens when you have experienced a miracle. You let people know, especially when it's something as dramatic as this—she couldn't move, and all of a sudden, she *can* move! My mom was *completely* healed—from that day until some time in 1995, about a year before I was ordained a priest. So for almost twenty years, my mom had no pain. The doctors couldn't explain it. All we knew was that God had dramatically broken into Mom's life.

In 1995, about as quickly as Mom's pain left, it all came back and became more intense than it had ever been before she had been healed. And that's how my mom has lived since then. People have prayed often for my mom to be healed. But my mom will tell you, in all honesty, that what she has is a gift. She knows God can heal her. He *did* heal her. And for whatever reason, he has chosen to bring this back to her. A lot of us think our moms are saints. But because of the witness of her life, I know that for me, it's true—my mom is a saint. People love to talk to her. She is the most amazing person, together with my dad, that I know. They are filled with wisdom.

## Suffering Is a Vocation

Here are the Scripture passages that have been most helpful to my mom as she lives with this pain every day of her life.

First, "Take up your cross and follow me" (cf. Mark 8:34; cf. Luke 9:23; cf. Matthew 16:24). I'm not sure what we think today when we hear that verse, but for a first-century Jew, we certainly know what *they* thought. First-century Jews were used to seeing crucifixions. "The cross" was no figure of speech. The cross was the manner of execution for the rebels in the area, a way for the Romans to show off, boast of their power, and make their authority felt. So when Jesus tells us to pick up our cross and follow him, he's clearly trying to make it known to us that this is going to entail hardships of a variety of different kinds.

Alluding to this passage, here is what St. John Paul II said:

People react to suffering in different ways. But in general it can be said that almost always the individual enters suffering with a *typically human protest* and *with the question "why."* He asks the meaning of his suffering and seeks an answer to this question on the human level. Certainly he often puts this question to God, and to Christ. Furthermore, he cannot help noticing that the one to whom he puts the question is himself suffering and wishes *to answer him* from the Cross, *from the heart of his own suffering.* Nevertheless, it often takes time, even a long time, for this answer to begin to be interiorly perceived. For Christ does not answer directly and he does not answer in the abstract this human questioning about the meaning of suffering. Man hears Christ's saving answer as he himself gradually becomes a sharer in the sufferings of Christ.

The answer which comes through this sharing, by way of the interior encounter with the Master, is in itself *something more than the mere abstract answer* to the question about the meaning of suffering. For it is above all a call. It is a vocation. Christ does not explain in the abstract the reasons for suffering, but before all else he says: "Follow me!" Come! Take part through your suffering in this work of saving the world, a salvation achieved through my suffering! Through my Cross. Gradually, *as the individual takes up his cross*, spiritually uniting himself to the Cross of Christ, the salvific meaning of suffering is revealed before him. (*Salvifici Doloris*, 26)

Suffering is a vocation, and we will all be called to it if we haven't been already.

The second passage that my mom has found very helpful is the ending of Matthew 28, the Great Commission, when Jesus instructs the disciples to go out into all the world to preach and baptize. This is the last thing Jesus says: "I am with you always" (verse 20). That was the great promise of Christmas. God is Emmanuel—he is *with* us. He is *always* with us—no matter what. Nothing, nothing, can separate us from him.

The third passage is from St. Paul. As you might remember, Paul had this affliction, which is translated as a "thorn." It is really more like a "spike" in his flesh. There have been countless theologians and Scripture scholars who have speculated what it was. God hasn't chosen to reveal that to us. But it was something serious enough that Paul begged the Lord three times to take it from him. And this was the Lord's answer: "No." He told Paul, "My grace is sufficient for you, for my power is made perfect in weakness" (2 Corinthians 12:9).

And here's the last passage, which comes from Jesus' agony in the Garden of Gethsemane. As he is lying there sweating blood, he prays, "Father, if you are willing, remove this chalice from me; nevertheless not my will, but yours, be done" (Luke 22:42). When we are grieving, when we are suffering, when we are in the midst of trying to discover the meaning of what's going on, when we can't think of anything else to do but throw ourselves on the ground, we cry out to the Lord, "Not my will, but yours, be done." Still, to be a Christian is not to be a masochist. We do ask him to take away our suffering. We ask the Lord to heal us.

## Counting on God's Grace

When I asked my mother what she would like others to come away with, here is what she said. "First, I would want them to recognize how absolutely weak I am, we all are, to change things." My mom lives in pain twenty-four hours a day, seven day a week, 365 days a year. She gets no relief. The doctors can find nothing to help her. When I get sick—when I get a cold or the flu—I am secure in the hope that one day I'm going to feel better. Like others who suffer with chronic pain, my mom has no such illusions. She is going to go to bed. She is going to sleep an hour or two, and when she wakes up, she is going to hurt. When we get a headache or a migraine, we pop a couple of pills, go to bed, and hope we feel better when we wake up. And we usually are, and then we go about our day, which gives us the illusion that we can change things. But in reality, we are absolutely powerless to change things.

Second, the only thing we can count on is God's grace, that is to say, his strength and his power, which he has promised is enough. Just as he said to St. Paul, he says to us, "My grace is sufficient for you, for my power is made perfect in weakness." There is nothing that anyone is going through that God doesn't give the grace, the strength, to go through. That doesn't mean it's romantic. It's not. But there's grace for it at the time we are suffering. We often hear about a very difficult situation, and we say to ourselves, "If that happened to me, I don't know how I'd get through it." Well, of course we don't, because God only gives us the grace we need at the time we are going through the trial. What we have to do is trust that he will give those whom we love the grace that they need to get through their suffering.

This is a really subtle temptation that the evil one uses on parents, especially on moms: to doubt that God will give his grace to help their children who are suffering. After all, a good mom always wants to protect her children. What kind of mom, or any parent, wouldn't want to do that? But the evil one worms his way into our thinking and twists and perverts it so that we forget that God will give to our children, whatever their age, the grace they need. Yet he's not giving *us* that grace; he is giving *them* that grace. And we have to trust that God will take care of them and provide for them, and that he will break into their lives even if it's not the way we think he should. Grace is sufficient, always, all the time. God is always faithful.

The third point my mom wanted to emphasize is that faith is a gift, and without it, we can't go anywhere. With it, we can do anything. With faith, with God's work in us to which we respond (remember, that's the definition of faith), we can do anything and go anywhere. But without it, relying on ourselves, we're doomed.

As I said before, my mom is a classy, elegant woman, and she likes to look nice. We all like to look nice; we find a sense of worth in that. And when we look nice, we feel better. My mom can't look as nice as she'd like to look any longer. She can't do herself up the way she'd like. And this is the last thing she wanted me to share with you. The Lord has taught her that just as she is, God loves her. Just as you and I are, God loves us. And nothing can take that from her, or from us. And that's what keeps us from fear and anxiety. She has learned, in a way that only a lesson in suffering can teach us, that God really doesn't care about the things we think are important, such as how we look, what kind of shape we're in, whether we're "healthy"—all those things that the world prizes, enshrines, and idolizes. God is not impressed because God doesn't see appearances; he looks into the heart.

## The Meaning of Suffering

Viktor Frankl was a Holocaust survivor who went on to become a famous therapist. He invented a therapy he coined "Logotherapy," which basically means "meaning therapy." He was trying to figure out why it was that people survived the death camps. One of the things he observed from his own experience, which he describes in his famous book *Man's Search for Meaning*, was that those people who had something to live for found the means by which they could endure the concentration camp. And those who didn't were much more likely to give up and die. What he said can be summed up in a quasi-mathematical expression: suffering minus meaning equals despair.

Think about Good Friday. Close your eyes and imagine that you are in Jerusalem. Try to picture yourself walking through a dusty, hot, and noisy street that is rich with the smell of spices in the air. Listen to the uproar and the din that come from hearing someone being publicly executed. If you and I had been there on that Friday, what would we have thought? Just another crucifixion, another show of Roman power, another meaningless death, a man cut down in his prime. What possible good could come of this? What a waste! And yet, of course, the truth is absolutely different. Because, as the great twentieth-century Catholic apologist Frank Sheed stressed, on that cross Jesus "was active as no man has ever been."[10]

The only way you can nail God to a cross is if he wills to be there. You and I can't find nails that can nail God to a cross. The only way Jesus could have been hanging there was because he wanted to be there. He was not being passive when he was suffering. He was being active, more active than when he healed the paralytic, more active than when he calmed the storm, more active than when he raised Lazarus from the dead, more active than when he multiplied the fish and loaves. It was the most active he had ever been during his time on earth. And on that cross and in that suffering, he was saving the world. Because the world wasn't saved by the multiplication of the loaves, by the calming of the storm, or by the raising of Lazarus; it was saved by his passion. And we, too, can share in that redemption. Pope St. John Paul wrote,

> The Redeemer suffered in place of man and for man. Every man has *his own share in the Redemption*. Each one is also *called to share in that suffering* through which . . . all human suffering has also been redeemed. In bringing about the Redemption through suffering, Christ *has also raised human suffering to the level of the Redemption*. Thus each man, in his suffering, can also become a sharer in the redemptive suffering of Christ. (*Salvifici Doloris*, 19)

And that, my brothers and sisters, is the meaning of suffering. When St. Paul says he completes up in his own flesh what is lacking in the sufferings of Christ, he is *not* trying to say, "If Jesus could have hung on for only a few more hours, his suffering would have been complete." The only thing lacking in the sufferings of Christ is our participation in it. And *when,* not *if*, suffering comes our way, we can either unite it to his cross or we can do what I often do, which is to just complain.

At a convocation of the priests of our archdiocese recently, the archbishop gave a very candid address to all of the priests. At one point, he said this: "God wants his world back, and we have to help him." And nobody helps him get his world back any more than those of us who are suffering.

When you and I unite our suffering to the cross of Jesus, it is the greatest act of love we can make. Why? Because when we suffer, we are most inclined to be selfish. We hurt and we want others to care for us. But when we can instead unite our suffering to his cross for others, we help him "get his world back."

So what's our understanding of the reality? Jesus wants you and me to help him in his work of redeeming the world. That's the goal. Again, this is not romantic—I don't mean to try to put it that way. But for those of you who are sharing intimately right now in the cross of Jesus, whatever the outcome, know this: one day when you go home and stand in front of the Lord, he's going to look at you and say, "Let me show you the way I used that suffering." And you're going to be astounded.

So the meaning of suffering is to share in Jesus' cross. His dying on the cross was not in vain, even though it would have looked that way if you'd seen it on that Friday in Jerusalem. In the same way, the Lord wants to remind us that our suffering— whatever kind it is or will be—is never in vain when we unite it to the cross.

Let us pray:

*Father, we thank you for the cross of your Son. Through his death, you restored your friendship with us, reconciled us to one another and to ourselves, closed the gates of hell, and made possible our forgiveness. You transform our own suffering now in this life so that we can, in an act of love like his, unite it to all he endured for us and help you get your world back. Give us encouragement, especially those of us who are sharing intimately in the cross of Jesus. Protect us from any and all discouragement. Help us to know that no suffering is meaningless if it is united to the cross of Christ.*

*Mother Mary, you stood at the foot of that cross as the blood of your Son poured out upon you. Keep vigilant company, especially with those of us who most need your intercession and your strong maternal love and comfort. All of this we ask in Jesus' name. Amen.*

## QUESTIONS FOR REFLECTION AND DISCUSSION

1. What do you typically do when suffering comes your way?

2. What is your understanding of the reality that Jesus wants you to help him in his work of redeeming the world?

3. Think of a time when you were suffering and you turned to the Lord. (Whether you turned to him quickly or not doesn't matter.) Compare it to a time, maybe earlier in your life, when you suffered and didn't know Jesus in the same way, and you didn't turn to him. How did those experiences differ?

4. If you had been present on Good Friday, what would you have thought?

5. Do you really believe that no suffering united to Jesus' cross is in vain?

# CHAPTER 5

# *Greed*

As I've stressed previously, to say, "I want to begin to live the life of heaven *now*" is very different from saying, "I want to *get* to heaven." That's because we're convinced that the gospel is more, not less. Jesus has abundant life to offer us even now.

And we can discover that life by diving more deeply into his word so that we can obtain the freedom and fullness of the life he has promised us. It's so important to let the word of God form us. If we can drink deeply from the word of God, we can be formed by his word instead of being formed by the mentality of the world around us.

As we talk about the sin of greed or avarice and what we can learn from the Scriptures, here's something that may surprise you. You may already know there are seven capital sins. But do you know they have an order? The first capital sin is pride. How do you think lust is ranked? It's down toward the bottom; not last, but just ahead of gluttony. Where is greed? Second! Just behind pride and way ahead of lust comes greed.

The Bible has a lot to say about greed. Let's first begin with a definition. St. Thomas Aquinas says avarice is "the immoderate greed [or desire] of temporal possessions which . . . can be estimated in the value of money."[11] It's not the desire for temporal possessions; it is the immoderate desire—the disordered desire.

What is so dangerous about this? It's dangerous because it makes things into ends and into gods. That's a challenge for our culture. We all want the latest things—the newest version of the iPhone, the latest car. It's built into our culture that if we can only have this or that, we'll be happy.

But we know better. We know that such things won't make us happy, that there is something that is disordered within us that needs serious healing. Making things into ends is simply foolish. It assumes that happiness can come from possessing things. And happiness doesn't come from possessing things; happiness comes only from love. Your car can talk—maybe— but it can't love you. There's nothing wrong with such things in themselves; they just can't make us happy.

Having wealth also apes self-sufficiency. It tricks me, getting me to mistakenly think that I'm okay. I have enough, I'm taken care of, I can provide for myself.

## The Old Testament View

In the Old Testament, wealth is seen as a sign of God's blessing. Someone who is wealthy is understood to be prosperous because God has looked with favor upon that person. And yet at the same time, there is the constant exhortation from God to those with wealth to do good, especially to the poor, and to give God the first fruits of their labor.

Let's start briefly with a few Old Testament passages. First, Proverbs 3:9-10: "Honor the LORD with your substance / and with the first fruits of all your produce; / then your barns will be filled with plenty, / and your vats will be bursting with wine." This is one of the underlying themes in the Old Testament regarding money: God is constantly challenging the people to give to him first.

When I first started to think seriously about tithing some of my income, my dad was my model. He tithes an extraordinary percentage of his income, which I won't name because I don't want to embarrass him. But when the stock market crashed a few years ago and all the investments were going down, my dad called me in something of a panic. And his panic was over the fact that he might not be able to give as much as he had over past years. I'll admit, that would not have been my primary concern.

So the Scriptures are always kind of daring us: give to me first, the Lord says. That's not because the Lord needs money but because it's a very tangible way for us to show that we trust God. Even though our coins have inscribed on them "In God we trust," we really don't trust him. Instead, we trust in the coin and what we think the coin can do for us and how it can provide for us.

Malachi 3:10 echoes this same theme: "Bring the full tithes into the storehouse, that there may be food in my house; and thereby put me to the test, says the LORD of hosts, if I will not open the windows of heaven for you and pour down for you an overflowing blessing." This is a great dare from God: "Bring me everything you have; don't cheat me." Don't start off by saying, "What can I give God now that I've taken care of all of my needs?" Start by giving him your first fruits.

Another passage in the Old Testament, Ecclesiastes 5:10, has a different spin: "He who loves money will not be satisfied with money; nor he who loves wealth, with gain." Do we ever feel like we have enough? Do we ever get to that point? Yet some people continue to amass wealth no matter how much money they already have.

## What Does Jesus Say?

Jesus speaks more about the danger of riches than he speaks about any other sin. In the Gospels, we often find the apostles confused when Jesus talks about wealth. That's because they were coming from the Old Testament viewpoint that wealth was a sign of favor from God. Let's look at a few passages.

"For where your treasure is, there will your heart be also" (Matthew 6:21). That's a great verse because, first of all, it's short. You don't have to take a long time to actually read it or even memorize it. But it is a good text to reflect on in the course of a day and ask the Lord, "Show me where my treasure is because I want my heart to belong to you. I want my heart to be yours, and yet I'm mindful that there are all these other things that have a tug on my heart."

How do you know what your treasure is? Here is something to ask yourself: "What do I think about? What occupies all my attention?" Whatever it is, that is your treasure. For me, it's golf. For another priest I know, it's hunting. He once said to me, "Do you ever think about golf when you are saying Mass? Because sometimes I think about hunting when I'm saying Mass." It's sobering, but I was so encouraged to know that. I just have to lay that at the feet of Jesus and say, "Yes, Lord, just take that treasure from my heart."

Jesus also taught parables that warn us about wealth. In the parable of the sower and the seed (Matthew 13:1-7, 18-23), some seed fell on the path, some seed fell on rocky soil, some seed fell among thorns, and some seed fell on good soil. "As for what was sown among thorns, this is he who hears the word but the cares of the world and the delight in riches choke the word, and it proves unfruitful" (verse 22).

If we're not careful, riches can prevent us from doing what God wants us to do with our lives. Money can strangle us because we become preoccupied with gaining more, protecting what we have and what it can buy us. Then those things become ends in themselves and become dangers for us. We also fall into a pattern of self-sufficiency, looking to ourselves rather than to God.

## Blind to Reality

In the Gospel of Luke, a man asks Jesus to command his brother to divide the inheritance with him. Jesus responds with a warning and then a story about "the rich fool":

> "Take heed, and beware of all covetousness; for a man's life does not consist in the abundance of his possessions." And he told them a parable, saying, "The land of a rich man brought forth plentifully." (Luke 12:15-16)

Note the wording: the man didn't do anything; it was the land that brought him his bounty. This is just another way of the Lord reminding us that everything we have is a gift. Now, this isn't meant to slam those of us who work hard to gain what we get. But the truth is that everything I have is a gift—even the talent to be able to do what I do. To continue the parable:

> "And he thought to himself, 'What shall I do, for I have nowhere to store my crops?' And he said, 'I will do this: I will pull down

my barns, and build larger ones; and there I will store all my grain and my goods. And I will say to my soul, Soul, you have ample goods laid up for many years; take your ease, eat, drink; be merry.' But God said to him, 'Fool!'" (Luke 12:17-20)

We don't use the word "fool" very often today as a severe indictment, but in Scripture, a fool is one of the worst things that someone can be called. To be wise is to have the virtue of being able to see reality as it truly is—that is wisdom. Foolishness is the opposite of wisdom; foolishness is being blind to reality. To be a fool—to be blind to reality—is such an insult because it means that you don't know how to live; you don't know what it's all about. This man has mistakenly thought that it was all about storing up wealth. To put it in modern-day parlance, he lived by the slogan, "He who dies with the most toys wins." To which God says,

> "'This night your soul is required of you; and the things you have prepared, whose will they be?' So is he who lays up treasure for himself, and is not rich toward God." (Luke 12:20-21)

There's a legend about Alexander the Great that at his burial, he wanted to have his right hand outside of the sarcophagus so as to tell everyone, "You take nothing with you." But, as Jesus shows us, you do take something with you; you take what it is you have done.

At the end of the movie *Schindler's List*, there is a powerful image for how, I'm afraid, so many of us are going to look at our wealth. As the war is ending, the Russians are coming into Poland, and this man who has rescued so many Jewish people has to divest himself of all the things that just months ago were symbols of his prestige and protection. The great long dress coat, the beautiful car, the Nazi swastika gold pin—all these things he has to get rid of now because they don't help him; they accuse him.

Up until this time, he had been using much of his wealth to rescue Jewish men and women. He would bribe German officials to divert Jews who were supposed to be sent to a concentration camp to work in his factory instead. That's what he was doing with his life; it was really noble. But now he's got all these leftover possessions, and he is looking at them and doing what we may do at the end of our own lives—he is indicting himself. He looks at his pin and realizes that by selling that pin, he could have saved two more people. The car, ten more people. The coat, one more person. It's a great image to keep in mind with the stuff we have.

## Where Is Your Hope?

On what do we set our hope? It's easy to pin our hopes on money and what it can provide for us. 1 Timothy 6:17 says, "As for the rich in this world, charge them not to be haughty, nor to set their hopes on uncertain riches." Don't put your hopes in your IRA, your stocks, your home value; don't put your hopes in anything you have. Everything can be taken from us—all of it can be lost in a moment! Don't put your hopes on uncertain riches but on God who richly furnishes us with everything to enjoy. "They [the rich] are to do good, to be rich in good deeds, liberal and generous, thus laying up for themselves a good foundation for the future, so that they may take hold of the life which is life indeed" (6:18-19).

This life is a pilgrimage on the way home. It's all about living it in such a way that when we stand in front of the Lord—and we all will—he will say to us, "Well done" (Matthew 25:23), not "Depart from me" (25:41). The Lord is reminding us of what he will say to us at the end of our lives, depending on what we did with what we had.

In that regard, the parable of the rich man and Lazarus is another story we can reflect on (Luke 16:19-31). When the rich man stands in front of God, he is condemned to hell. What did he do? Nothing! The rich man did nothing. He didn't commit some gross offense; he committed a sin of omission. He didn't care for the poor man who was right outside his door, who was, in fact, the Lord in his distressing disguise. The rich man did nothing for that poor man, and the price of doing nothing was that he was condemned.

And that should sober us as we drive down the streets in our communities and see people in the streets with signs saying, "Homeless. Will work for food." As we sit there in our warm, comfortable cars, we might think, "That's probably just a scam." It might be. But I don't think when you and I die and stand face-to-face with the Lord, he will look at us and say, "I think you were way too generous; you were just too liberal with what you had."

Here's one last passage we can reflect on, taken from the Book of Revelation. Laodicea was an extremely wealthy community, renowned for its material resources and other things, which resulted in great pride. It was so wealthy that some time in the century or so before the letter was written, the city had been totally destroyed in an earthquake and was rebuilt without help from Rome.

"And to the angel of the Church in Laodicea write: 'The words of the Amen, the faithful and true witness, the beginning of God's creation.

"'I know your works: you are neither cold nor hot. Would that you were cold or hot! So, because you are lukewarm, and neither cold nor hot, I will spew you out of my mouth. For you say, I am rich, I have prospered, and I need nothing; not knowing that you are wretched, pitiable, poor, blind, and naked. Therefore I counsel you to buy from me gold refined by fire, that you may be rich, and white garments to clothe you and to keep the shame of your nakedness from being seen, and salve to anoint your eyes, that you may see. Those whom I love, I reprove and chasten; so be zealous and repent. Behold, I stand at the door and knock; if any one hears my voice and opens the door, I will come in to him and eat with him, and he with me.'" (Revelations 3:14-20)

This passage and others, such as James 5:1-6, are hard sayings. But we just want to hear the Lord speaking to us and understand that this is the Lord who loves us, who, because he loves us, speaks frankly and directly to us, trying to lead us to the path that brings life.

## The Remedy for Greed

What's the remedy for greed? I would start with the first beatitude: "Blessed are the poor in spirit, for theirs is the kingdom of heaven" (Matthew 5:3).

What in the world does Jesus mean by "blessed"? There are many different translations of that word, depending on the Bible you use. Among the best is a more poetic translation for "blessed," which would be something like "on the way." It's a word that expresses the idea of pilgrimage. We're all wayfarers in this life here; we are all journeying toward home. So we could say, "On the way home" or "On the way to heaven are the poor in spirit"; "On the way home are the pure of heart"; "On the way home are the peacemakers." Those who are blessed have already begun to live now the life of heaven, which is the goal we're aiming for.

Which "poor" does Jesus mean? Poor in spirit or just downright poor? Matthew says "poor in spirit," but Luke says "poor" (6:20).

Fr. Raniero Cantalamessa, who is the preacher to the papal household, says this: "Jesus certainly is concerned with the real poor, but that is not what he has in mind when he proclaims the poor 'blessed.' What he has in mind concerning the real poor is shown when he states that what is done—or not done—to them is done to him."[12] That reminds us of people like Lazarus sitting outside the rich man's door or the people in Matthew 25, who are sick or imprisoned or hungry or thirsty. What are we doing for them?

Cantalamessa goes on to say, "God does not value what the poor have but what they do not have." What don't the poor have? "Self-sufficiency, a closed attitude, a presumption of being able to save themselves. "[13] The poor are under no illusions that they can take care of themselves. We are under the illusion that we *can* take care of ourselves.

In chapter 3, when we talked about fear, we were looking at the passage of Jesus calming the storm at sea (Matthew 8:23-27) and made the point that the apostles were only in the storm because they had been following Jesus. If they hadn't followed Jesus, they wouldn't have been in the storm. One of the lessons from that miracle is that Jesus oftentimes leads us into storms so as to wake us up to the reality that we desperately need him.

We don't need him a little bit; we need him desperately. The poor know that. Those of us who are not poor oftentimes forget it. The poor are blessed because there's room in their hearts for the Lord. Here is what author Tadeusz Dajczer says in his book *The Gift of Faith*:

A person poor in spirit is one who is stripped of self-confidence. He is one who knows he cannot count on himself, on his own strength. . . . If you feel strong in your natural abilities, your faith cannot develop and deepen. That is why you have to experience your weakness; you have to realize that you cannot do some things. This will be the call to faith. Your weakness, inability, and helplessness will become a crack through which the grace of faith will squeeze into your heart.[14]

This is the challenge that Cantalamessa offers us: to be for the poor and to be poor. He wants us to avoid falling into one of two extremes. One extreme is to think that we all have to be poor and so we should sell all that we own (which we shouldn't do unless the Lord calls us to do it). The other extreme is to think that what counts is only how we use our money; that we don't have to become "poor" in a way that requires sacrifice or a stripping of our self-sufficient attitudes.

## Called to Help Others in Different Ways

The point here is that there's no universal way to live. There are a variety of charisms given to us. Scripture helps us to understand that the gift of liberality is a charism. This is from Paul's letter to the Romans:

> For as in one body we have many members, and all the members do not have the same function, so we, though many, are one body in Christ, and individually members one of another. Having gifts that differ according to the grace given to us, let us use them: if prophecy, in proportion to our faith; if service, in our serving; he who teaches, in his teaching; he who exhorts, in his exhortation; he who contributes, in his liberality; he who gives aid, with zeal; he who does acts of mercy, with cheerfulness. (12:4-8)

Paul is reminding us that the body has many parts, that not everyone teaches, not everyone exhorts, not everyone heals, not everyone has the means by which they can help others. But all of us, members of the same body, are called to use our gifts in such a way that the body can continue to grow to be what it is entitled to be or what it is entrusted to become.

Some people are, in fact, called to give away all that they own. St. Anthony (c. 251–356) was orphaned at a very young age and inherited tremendous wealth from his parents. He experienced a great conversion in his life. At the time, he was caring for his young unmarried sister. As he was wrestling with what he was supposed to be doing with all the wealth he had, he walked into church and heard the words of Jesus from the story of the rich young man: "If you would be perfect, go, sell what you possess and give to the poor, and you will have treasure in heaven; and come, follow me" (Matthew 19:21).

Anthony took that as confirmation that the Lord wanted him to get rid of everything. At first, he kept enough of his wealth to care for the poor around him and his sister. But he was wrestling even with that decision, and then he heard the Lord tell him, "Do not worry about tomorrow. Tomorrow will take care of itself" (cf. Matthew 6:34). So he disposed of all his wealth and put his sister in the care of a convent and went to live in the desert.

St. Barnabas, in Acts 4:36-37, does the same thing. He sells all his land, puts the money at the feet of the apostles, and goes on to do missionary work with them. In fact, one of the first things that is shown in the early chapters of the Acts of the Apostles, which radically defines the Christian community after the resurrection, is that people who have wealth get rid of their wealth. It's one of the strongest indicators of the proof of the resurrection of Jesus.

Why is this so? Because all of a sudden, these early Christians realized that the gold brick they had been holding was a paving stone to heaven. Because of the hope of eternal life with God forever, everything took on a different meaning for them and was valued in a different way. All the things that used to mean so much didn't mean so much anymore. They realized that the brick of gold had been given to them, certainly to provide for themselves and for others, but also to help and do good, to store up treasure in heaven.

So some people are called to sell everything. But others are called to use their resources to help those in need. Remember, it is the love of money, not money itself, that is the root of all evil (1 Timothy 6:10). I know some covetous, selfish poor people, and I know some extraordinarily generous wealthy people who actually feel guilty over the wealth they have. And because of their guilt, they are constantly trying to give it away. And perhaps because they're constantly trying to give it away, God just keeps putting more and more into their hands, because he knows he can trust them with it. It's not a trap for them; it's not a snare, so he just keeps blessing them with more.

So it's not that having wealth is *bad*. However, Jesus speaks very frankly that having wealth is *dangerous*. We noted that in the Old Testament, the wealthy were thought to be those who were blessed by God. Jesus totally turns that upside down when he tells the rich young man what he needs to do to find eternal life: "Go, sell all your possessions. Give to the poor, and you will have treasure in heaven. Then come follow me" (cf. Mark 10:17-22).

Some people truly are called to divest themselves of everything out of love for the poor. That's not necessarily what we are called to do. But we are called to examine our consciences and our lives to see if greed has any place in our hearts. How can we be truly generous in every area of our lives? What are we doing with the material blessings that the Lord has given us?

At the end of the marriage rite, there is a blessing before the dismissal when the celebrant says, "May you be ready and willing to help and comfort all who come to you in need." God has given us material gifts to provide for ourselves, and there is nothing wrong with that. But we want to be sure that we are storing up treasures in heaven, "where no thief approaches and no moth destroys" (Luke 12:33).

## Questions for Reflection and Discussion

1. What's my treasure? (Hint: it's whatever consumes your thoughts.)

2. How can I live more simply in this materialistic culture?

3. How can I join with my parish community to be better "for the poor"?

# CHAPTER 6

# *Surrender*

S o far we have looked seriously at some of the dimensions of the life of heaven that we can really live now. In this chapter, we are going to address the issue of surrender, which is the lynchpin between where we've gone so far and where we're going. This is a time of serious decision-making. It's a clarion call to take our hands off the wheel of our lives.

There's going to be a lot of "the's" in this chapter: *the* text, *the* prayer, *the* book, *the* model.

The text is Romans 12:1: "I appeal to you therefore, brethren, by the mercies of God, *to present your bodies as a living sacrifice*, holy and acceptable to God, which is your spiritual worship" (emphasis added).

The prayer is the prayer of abandonment by Blessed Charles de Foucault, who died in 1916. I find it to be the single most difficult prayer to pray. I can't always pray it. In all honesty, I find it much more difficult than the line in the Our Father where we ask God to "forgive us our trespasses as we forgive those who trespass against us." Here it is:

Father,
I abandon myself into your hands;
do with me what you will.
Whatever you may do, I thank you:
I am ready for all, I accept all.

Let only your will be done in me,
and in all your creatures—
I wish no more than this, O Lord.

Into your hands I commend my soul:
I offer it to you with all the love of my heart,
for I love you, Lord, and so need to give myself,
to surrender myself into your hands without reserve,
and with boundless confidence,
for you are my Father.

The book is called *Into Your Hands, Father: Abandoning Ourselves to the God Who Loves Us*, written by a Belgian Carmelite priest, Fr. Wilfrid Stinissen. It's an exceptional book that I've read several times now. In many ways, it's a commentary on the prayer of abandonment.

The model is Jesus. Jesus' life is one of surrender, not just his earthly life, but the life of the Trinity. When we celebrate Trinity Sunday after Pentecost, we wonder how there can be three Persons in one God. We might think, "What an abstract principle—I can't relate to it." But there's nothing more important for us to understand. Why? Because you and I are made in the image and likeness of God. So it's only to the degree that we understand something about God that we will ever understand who we're supposed to be.

Who is God? Here is the most basic thing we can say about God: "God is three"—three Persons—who live perpetually in a life of reckless self-giving. That's God's life; God pours himself out. The Father pours himself out to the Son, and the Son pours himself back out to the Father. The love that is the relationship between the Father and the Son is so intense that it's another Person: the Holy Spirit.

What does that mean for us? It means that we will find fulfillment to the degree that we live like God. And how does God live? With reckless self-giving. So when we say that Jesus is the model, it's not just as Jesus lived his earthly life and went to the cross. This is, if you will, a picture of how the eternal Son of God has always lived. He gives everything back to the Father. That's our model.

Quoting Psalm 40, the author of Hebrews writes that this is what Christ said when he came into the world: "Sacrifices and offerings you have not desired, / but a body you have prepared for me; / in burnt offerings and sin offerings you have taken no pleasure. / Then I said, 'Behold, I have come to do your will, O God'" (10:5-7). That's Jesus' life.

And remember Jesus' words at the Garden of Gethsemane: "And he [Jesus] withdrew from them about a stone's throw, and knelt down and prayed, Father, if you are willing, remove this chalice from me; nevertheless not my will, but yours, be done'" (Luke 22:41-42). So Jesus is the model.

Here's another "the"—the perfect disciple, Mary. She lived just like Jesus and shows us what it means to be conformed to him. Mary said to the angel Gabriel, "Behold I am the handmaid of the Lord; let it be to me according to your word" (Luke 1:38).

## A Living Sacrifice

Let's go back to the text: "I appeal to you therefore, brethren, by the mercies of God, to present your bodies as a living sacrifice" (Romans 12:1). "Bodies" here doesn't just mean the physical stuff we are made of. For a Jewish person or a Jewish understanding of Scripture, there is no separation of what it means to have a body; we are a body and a soul together. It's one word in Hebrew, *nephesh*, better understood as "body-soul." You are not a body inhabited with a soul; you are not a soul that's imprisoned in a body. Those are Greek ways of thinking, not Christian or Jewish ways of thinking.

What is a living sacrifice? It's literally a living killing. This is what Paul is urging us: "Present yourselves to God as a living killing." Paul is writing to a culture, obviously, that is very familiar with sacrifice, whether it is the Jewish sacrifices that took place in the Temple or the pagan sacrifices that took place in all the various temples in the ancient world. When we hear the word "sacrifice," we think of giving something up. But when those in the first-century pagan-Christian world heard the word "sacrifice," they thought of an animal being killed.

There are some similarities and some differences between the sacrifices of old and what Paul is urging us to do. What are the differences? The biggest difference is this: in the Old Testament, you take an animal, you put it on an altar, you take a knife, you slit its throat, and it's gone, it's dead. However, you are not; you just keep living. It's a living killing. In a sermon, the Protestant pastor Timothy Keller quotes another minister as saying, "The trouble with a living sacrifice is that it keeps crawling off the altar."[15] And we do the same, right? I begin my prayer, my holy hour every morning, by saying, "Lord, here I am. I'm crawling back on top of the altar again this morning. I'm yours." But we have to do this again and again. And yet doing this—and this is really the key—is what leads to life. We can't lose sight of that.

What are the similarities between the sacrifices of old and what Paul is encouraging us to do? One similarity is that something really dies. But as Keller points out, whether or not we are following Jesus, we all presenting ourselves to something or someone as a living sacrifice.[16]

What are we living for? What are we giving ourselves to? Are you giving yourself for a career? There are people who attack their careers with a fervor that puts Christians to shame. They stay up later than everyone else. They get up earlier than everyone else. Why? To get the degree, to get the job, to earn money. Which will get them what? Nothing, in the grand scheme of things. Because that doesn't satisfy us; it's not what we're made for. So we do this already; some of us are living sacrifices for our careers.

Or we might be living for our spouse—not loving our spouse but living for our spouse. Or living for our children, or for honors, or any of a variety of things. But if it's not God that we're sacrificing our bodies to, then to whatever or to whomever we are offering ourselves is eventually going to do one of two things: disappoint us or crush us. Because none of those things, good as they all are, are what we are made for. That's why everything has to be in the proper order.

So Paul is urging us to surrender, to present ourselves, to abandon ourselves, to *Someone* who is unbelievably good and unbelievably trustworthy. Here's the proof: no one loves us as God loves us. No one has given us a reason to surrender ourselves to that person as he has. In that prayer of abandonment, the operative word is *"Father."* Not just the generic

"God," but *Father*. Father implies relationship; Father means I'm his child.

## Your Father Knows What You Need

Remember in chapter 3, when we looked at what Jesus said in the Sermon on the Mount—do not fear like the pagans (cf. Matthew 6:31-32)? What are the pagans like? The pagans don't know there is a God. The pagans don't know someone cares. The pagans don't know that the God who made everything is a Father who loves them beyond all telling. They don't know that. But we do! Don't be like them; don't be afraid. Your Father knows what you need.

For those of you who are parents, the Lord allows you to participate in a remarkable way in an understanding of what it means to love another person. You didn't create your children. You procreated them; you cooperated with God in bringing life. So if you understand love in such a way—and you do—it helps you to understand something of what the Lord's love is like. And given such a love, you and I can trust God.

The fact is that everything we are doing is a response to a love that God has already shown. It's not as if we just live a great life, present it to God, and say, "Here it is. What do you think? Am I pleasing now?" Because then I'm afraid that as I live my life, God is standing above me with an anvil waiting for me to screw up, and as soon as I do, he drops it on me. But that's not God. Scripture tells us that God loved us first (1 John 4:19). Everything we do is a response to what God has done for us. Surrender is a response to what God has already done, not an attempt to win him over. You don't have to win him over, and you can't win him over. There's nothing you can do to make him love you more than he already does.

But we need to be clear, and this is the reason why this issue is so decisive. In a sacrifice, something dies. What dies? Here's how Keller puts it: "*What it means to live a Christian life is that you put to death the right to live life as you choose.*"[17] And if you don't feel punched in the gut by that sentence, then read it again. You can't live as you want. Neither can I. Not if we are going to be disciples, not if we are longing for sanctification. God's will is our sanctification—to have him take possession of our lives. It's just that when you hear it said that way, you realize how high the cost is.

Here is what Fr. Stinissen writes:

There can be so much escapism in our striving for a "spiritual life." We often flee from the concrete, apparently banal reality that is filled with God's presence to an artificial existence that corresponds with our own ideas of piety and holiness but where God is not present. As long as we want to decide for ourselves where we will find God, we need not fear that we shall meet him! We will meet only ourselves, a touched-up version of ourselves. Genuine spirituality begins when we are prepared to die.[18]

Could there be a quicker way to die than to let God form our lives from moment to moment and continually consent to his action in us? Fr. Stinissen goes on to say,

The Gospels and spiritual literature point out various practices of importance on the journey to God. We are told to deny ourselves, forgive one another, carry our cross, fast, and give alms. We must also love our neighbor, pray with others and in private, bring our troubles to the Lord, and be peacemakers. All of these things have their place, and nothing may be overlooked, but they may cause us to feel confused and divided, and we might even ask ourselves where we will find the strength to do all that is required. In spiritual reading we are instructed about balanced asceticism, the Mass readings of the day tell of prayer, and the retreat master speaks about love. We are pulled in different directions, and, instead of finding peace, we become restless. What we need most is a central idea, something so basic and comprehensive that it encompasses everything else. In my opinion that central idea is surrender. . . .

The life of Jesus shows that it is acceptable to choose surrender as a unifying idea. . . . Abandonment is truly the alpha and omega in his life.[19]

"Abandon" comes from an old French word that has the sense of "giving in to the control of another." People sometimes say to me, "I would like to be a Christian, but will I have to do this or that?" Jesus himself tells us to count the cost of discipleship. Someone comes up to him and says, "I'll follow you wherever you go." And Jesus says, "Foxes have holes, and birds of the air have nests; but the Son of man has nowhere to lay his head" (Luke 9:57, 58). Later on in that passage, a would-be disciple says, "I will follow you, Lord; but let me first say farewell to those at my home." Jesus says, "No one who puts his hand to the plow and looks back is fit for the kingdom of God" (9:61, 62).

It's almost as if Jesus is discouraging us from following him. He is reminding us over and over again, "Do you know what I'm asking of you? Yes, I have abundant life, but here's the key: in order to have abundant life, you have to have intimacy, and you can't have intimacy with me without surrendering to me." In fact, you can't have intimacy with anyone without surrendering to that person. Those of you who are married know that. Anyone with a real friend knows that. There's no such thing as intimacy without surrender.

So Jesus is telling us to count the cost. But I'm afraid that many people want to negotiate the cost rather than count it. That is, they are willing to give up things, but they won't give up the right to determine what those things are. They want to be in a position to do an ongoing cost-benefit analysis of various kinds of behavior. And that keeps them in the driver's seat, on the throne of their lives, as it were.

If you really want Jesus in the middle of your life, you have to obey him unconditionally. You have to give up control of your life and drop your conditions. You have to give up the right to say, "I will obey you if . . . " "I will do this if . . . " As soon as you say, "I will obey you if," that's not obedience. What you are really saying is this: "You are my consultant, not my Lord."

Sometimes, even when we want to surrender ourselves to the Lord, we get hung up on our past. And that is one of the things we have to abandon. We might think, "You know what, I have some ugly things in my past. I have to get my life in order before I can really do this." But how are you going to get your life in order without God?

Paul says in Philippians, "Forgetting what lies behind and straining forward to what lies ahead, I press on toward the goal for the prize of the upward call of God in Christ Jesus" (3:13-14). Remember what Paul is turning his back on: murder. You think you have memories in *your* past? What do you think Paul's memories are? Have you ever heard someone being stoned to death? Heard it, seen it, had the blood splatter on you? He did as he presided over the stoning of Stephen (Acts 7:54-60).

Forget about your past. If you have repented and been to Confession, it's gone; it's in the past. God doesn't remember it, so why do we? Have nothing to do with it. Jesus once said something along these lines to St. Catherine of Siena, "Don't you ever look at your sin and your past without looking at my cross. Because if you do, it will crush you."[20] Anytime the evil one holds up in front of us what's in our past, don't go there. Go to the cross and say, "Lord, I have repented of that already."

## Three Stages of Surrender

Fr. Stinissen outlines three stages of surrender, or abandonment, that can help us. Let's take a quick look at them.

The first stage is simply to accept and consent to God's will as it is revealed to us in the circumstances of our lives. This is what he calls the passive stage. "There is not a single moment," he writes, "when God is not communicating himself to us."[21] God has been with us in the midst of all the experiences we have gone through in our lives, all the great, good things and all the really terrible, traumatic things. This is not to say that God wanted those difficult things to happen. It is saying that there is not a single moment in which God has not been present, in which he has not been revealing something of himself to us and speaking to us. Most of what occurs in our lives seems to happen accidentally and at random. Now and then, God reveals his presence. At times we see the thread, and we thank him. But he's always there. Everything, all the time, everywhere, speaks of God, even creation. As the psalmist says, "The heavens are telling the glory of God" (19:1). Everything reveals God—all the events that happen in our lives, even those that people willed for evil.

Think of Joseph in the Old Testament. His brothers hate him. They sell him into slavery. He is sent to Egypt, the world power at the time. A married woman is attracted to him and tries to sleep with him. He won't do it, so she frames him. He gets sent to jail. Things couldn't get worse for this guy. What does God do?

God raises up Joseph through several circumstances, and he becomes the second most powerful person in Egypt. When there is a famine in the Middle East, everyone comes to Egypt because the Egyptians are the ones with the food. And who comes to Egypt asking this man for food? His brothers! But they don't know it's Joseph. And at a certain point, after hiding his identity for so long, Joseph finally looks at them and says, "Brothers, it's me! What you intended for evil, God has used for great good" (cf. Genesis 45:3-8). God is always there. Everything speaks for him—even evil. Everything that happens has a purpose in God's plan. He is so good that all that comes in contact with him becomes, in some way, good.

As Fr. Stinissen quotes St. Augustine, "God accomplishes his good will through the evil will of others."[22] He would not have permitted evil to occur if he had not, thanks to his perfect goodness, been able to use it. And here is the supreme example: "Take my son, nail him to a cross, and wait until you see what I do with it. I will save you through it."

## Obedience to God's Will

The second stage of surrender is being obedient to God's will, being his obedient servant. This is more active. The first stage is seeing God in everything that happens in our lives—in all the circumstances and events. But this second stage is actually doing God's will. We obediently carry out what he gives us to do. We put our hand to the plow and we get to work. Jesus invites us to follow his path of obedience with him and in the same way that he did.

If we ask a mature Christian to speak about his journey with God, it will always be a story of obedience, though the word itself may not be used. The mature Christian has said yes to God, and at certain times, he has probably said a more conscious, decisive, and perhaps more dramatic yes, which has borne fruit and has led him to say yes again and again. Without a yes to God, nothing can mature in a person's life. If one's life is barren, the reason behind it is always the frequent repetition of the word "no."

Mary is the model for this active obedience. Psalm 123:2 says, "Behold, as the eyes of servants / look to the hand of their master, / as the eyes of the maid / to the hand of her mistress, / so our eyes look to the LORD our God." Stinissen writes, "That is how Mary lived, with her eyes continually turned toward God. Her gaze was one single question: 'What would you have me do?'"[23] This doesn't mean insignificant things such as, "Lord, should I put pepper on my omelet or not?" I mention that because we often get scrupulous about these things.

If we are honest with ourselves, we know where we stand and we know the obstacles to obedience that we struggle with. In order to obey God, we must daily be striving to listen to him. We must not simply say prayers; we have to pray. What's the difference? When I pray, my heart is involved. It is much harder to pray than just to say prayers. I am guilty often of just saying prayers. Words are being said, but my heart is nowhere near to God's. That's the image for saying prayers versus praying. When my heart is engaged with the Lord, I'm really listening to him, and I'm pouring out what's going on in my life. If I don't regularly, daily, persistently, and intentionally strive to listen to the Lord about everything in my life, then it's no wonder that when I have a big decision and go to him, I have a hard time hearing him. I have not accustomed my ears to his voice. Here is what Fr. Stinissen says:

Many turn to God only when they must make an important or definitive choice in life. They approach God as a computer, so to speak, who gives answers to certain questions. . . . Writes Martin Lönnebo, . . . "Often we do not get a clear answer when we ask God questions in prayer. We can stand there just as perplexed after prayer as before. The secret of evangelical freedom from care is not that we surrender our life to God only at certain times. The secret is rather that we never leave God!" . . .

If our sense of obedience has not developed by a continual assent to God's clear and certain will, we cannot count on being able to perceive his will when we find ourselves before a difficult and unclear choice.[24]

We're not trying to say here that God wants us to obey him as if we are a machine or a puppet on a string. Remember who this is, who is talking to us and whom we are talking to. It's the God who made us, the Lord and lover of our souls, the One who died for us, the One who made us to be divinized and to share in his own life. When God wants us to do a certain work, it becomes meaningful and dear to us. We ought to love "it"—the work that he is asking us to do—with the same love with which we love God.

## God Working through Me

In the third stage of surrender, God does his willing through me. In the second stage, it is I who do God's will. I do it for him. In the third stage, he uses me; he does it *through* me.

St. Paul defines himself over and over again as a slave of the Lord. In antiquity, a slave was understood to be a "living tool." That's how Paul sees himself. It's not "I want to be a slave to the Lord and I want my own freedom." No, when you are a slave, you are a slave to someone or something else.

There ought to come a time, in the life of every Christian, when he is merely God's instrument and nothing more. In the third stage, surrender is much more radical and "total" than in the second. There I refrain from choosing for myself what I will do. I tred to discover God's will and then carry it out, but it was *I* who did God's will. Now I offer to God not only my will but also all my potential, all the powers of my soul, so that he himself may carry out his will through me.

This stage presupposes that we have practiced the first two stages, accepting and obeying God's will, for a long time. But we can't just say this third stage is for the elite, and the rest of us will just coast by in the first two stages. If we're serious about the life of discipleship, this is what we strive for. This is the goal; this is what sanctification looks like; this is letting God have possession of our lives. This is the image that Stinissen uses:

> Before, it was I who played the violin. It was God, of course, who gave me the score, and I obediently played what he gave me to play. Now I give the violin to God and let him play. One hears that it is the same violin. It has the same characteristics and defects. But there is no similarity between the music I produced myself and what resonates now. God not only makes use of all the violin's possibilities, but he reveals something of himself in its playing. It is that I have become more skilled. No, now an artist of the very highest grade is playing.
>
> Being God's violin is something completely different from playing the violin for God. Now he does not content himself with deciding what I should play, but he himself touches the strings of my faculties. He can do that only when he has the violin in his hands, when my surrender applies, not just to one part of myself, but to my whole self.[25]

Remember the prayer of abandonment: I abandon myself into God's hands. I offer the prayer to him with all the love of my heart, and so I need to give myself, to surrender myself, into his hands without reserve.

This is what you do when you marry someone. You are overwhelmed by the love of another person, and you say, "I have to, in response to the love you have shown me, give myself to you. There is no other logical thing to do. I surrender myself to you." So we have experience at this. But in marriage, we are surrendering ourselves to a man or woman who is flawed, as all of us are. When we surrender ourselves to God, we are surrendering ourselves to Someone who has loved us in an indescribable way. Indescribable, except for the fact that he described his love for us by going to the cross.

We do what God does and has always done when we surrender. The Father gives his whole life to the Son. The Son gives it back to the Father. The Spirit is himself this life that is given and poured out. To give one's life is to die. Here is one last quote from Stinissen:

> For many, death is the moment when life is taken away from them, the moment when God, who himself wants to be our life, finally conquers the insubordinate person and deprives him of that life which in his greed he seized and made his own, though it was and should have remained God's. As a rule, God must use a little force, because man resists right up to the end. Why wait so long with what must happen anyway and which becomes tremendously richer when it is done willingly? Why not say with Jesus: "No one takes [my life] from me, but I lay it down of my own accord" (John 10:18)? [26]

## QUESTIONS FOR REFLECTION AND DISCUSSION

1. We are urged to make of ourselves a living sacrifice to God in response to all he has done for us. To what am I making myself a sacrifice right now?

2. Do I have a real friendship with God and not just a once-a-week get-together for an hour on Sundays? What's my life of prayer *really* like?

3. Who are my biblical heroes of abandonment, and why? What did they have to abandon in their past in order to surrender to God?

# CHAPTER 7

# *Praise and Worship*

So far we have looked at fear, suffering, greed, and our struggle to forgive and to surrender our lives to the Lord. These are all issues that can act as obstacles that prevent us from reaching the Omega—our sanctification. In this chapter, I want to focus our attention on something that is a significant part of heaven and that we are able to experience right now: praise, or worship, and, perhaps in a more inclusive fashion, celebration.

The reality is that all of us are made to worship. We are made to praise. We are made to celebrate. And we do; we all do. We all worship lots of different things. We all praise lots of different things. We all celebrate lots of different things. We do it all the time and in various ways. We do it at sporting events, at concerts, at significant life events, and in the theater. We are inundated with a culture that praises and worships celebrity and personality cult. That is indisputable, I think.

I love college basketball. One year I happened to be in Atlanta for the Final Four, when the University of Michigan was playing, where I went to school. I had given up watching basketball for Lent that year, so I hadn't made the connection that I was going to be in Atlanta during the Final Four game until I actually walked off the plane and saw the TV screens. Then I called up my dad to see if he could get me a ticket—which he did.

If you've ever been to a Final Four game, there really is almost nothing like it, especially if the team from where you happened to go to school is playing in it. That Saturday night Michigan beat Syracuse. It was a blast! People were *ecstatic*.

It was a great night. It made for a great diversion and for some wonderful bragging rights. But so what? It didn't *do* anything for me. It didn't change reality. It didn't change the fact that some people I love dearly are very sick or that someone I was really close to had died recently. It was just a bunch of guys running around on a hardwood floor bouncing a leather ball. It's a *game*. It's celebratory, and it has its place, but it's a game.

And so as we examine the following Scripture passages, I hope I can help you to see the Lord in his goodness. I hope you can get a glimpse of his beauty and recognize how just and right it is for us to worship him. As saints, that's what we are called to do.

As we put on a biblical vision, I think it's going to be fairly difficult to come away with the conclusion that somehow we're actually doing what the Scriptures tell us we should do with regard to praise, worship, and celebration. I often say that there is a huge distinction between singing and worshipping. Many people come to Mass on Sunday and sing, but not everyone worships.

You want to see worship? You go to a Final Four basketball game or a rock concert. You see people involved with their whole hearts, bodies, and souls. And tragically, many of those people put us, who are disciples of the King of kings, to shame.

So who is, or what is, most deserving of our celebration, of our praise, of our worship? The operative word here is "justice." Justice is to give to someone what they are due. Injustice is to deprive someone of what they are due. Ask yourself: who is more deserving of our praise and worship than God? Who has done anything for us that can compare to what God has done for us?

Of course, when we worship God, we shouldn't be throwing our seat cushions in the air as they did at that Final Four game. But there is something we can learn from our experiences in the world. When we come to worship the King of kings, the Creator of heaven and earth, the One who has given me hope, who has conquered death, who has forgiven all my sins, we think we should somehow be straitjacketed and put in a box. As we dive into Scripture, we are going to see how that is a very unbiblical way of thinking.

I'm not saying that we all have to become charismatic. The beauty of Catholicism is that there is such a broad openness to a variety of spiritualities. You can be a cloistered Carmelite, a silent Trappist who never utters a word, or a charismatic. You can follow Ignatian or Franciscan spirituality. Even though the Church is one, there is so much diversity. It is just not true that we have to worship one way or another.

The only thing we have to do if we want to be a disciple of Christ, to be a saint, is to surrender, because I can't be a disciple and not surrender. So if you ask, "Do I have to become a charismatic?" the answer is no. But if you are going to be serious about following the Lord, you have to be open to whatever gifts he might want to give you. And he gives lots of gifts, and some of them are charismatic. We can't say to the Lord, "I'll take any gift, except *that*, and I certainly don't want *that*." We are not open to following the Lord if we say to him, "Lord, I'll do whatever you want, *but* . . . "

## What Is Prayer?

Let me first say something about prayer. We all know that we should be praying, but often we are just looking for something practical that shows us how to pray. We might want to know, for example, what prayer really is. What do we do? Are we just supposed to sit still and do nothing? That sounds really boring, so we don't want to do it.

Is the goal of prayer just to be silent? Or is the goal of prayer communication? What if you and I are trying to talk, and I'm watching something on TV at the same time? You say, "Hey, Father, are you listening to me?" I reply, "Yes." And you say, "No, you're not. You're watching the TV. Turn it off." I have to silence the other voices in order to be able to get into a dialogue with you. And that is the goal in prayer: to get into a dialogue with God, not to be still or to somehow become one with eternal nothingness. The goal is to hear the voice of God and be able to speak to him about whatever it is that's going on in our lives.

Prayer is not just saying words or saying prayers but praying. There's nothing wrong with saying prayers, but the difference between saying prayers and praying is that when I'm praying, my heart is involved. It is so easy to just say prayers and have my heart be a million miles away.

Pope St. John Paul II used to talk often about how a parish has to become what he referred to as "a school of prayer." We have to be more intentional about teaching people how to pray. Think about how you learned to pray. Prayer is not necessarily intuitive. I had it modeled for me by my mom, my dad, my siblings, and then by some men that I met when I was in college. It was extremely helpful to me.

How did you learn to pray? Just think about that. How do you pray? What do we do when we pray? Here are five ways to pray:

*Thanksgiving.* We thank God for what he's done for us.

*Intercession.* We lift up to God all the petitions we have—for ourselves, for those we love, and for the world. We should even be praying for our political leaders, which is something that Scripture exhorts us to do. A lot of us complain about political leaders, but how many of us *pray* daily for them?

*Repentance.* This should be a daily part of my prayer. Coming before the Lord, we say, "Lord, I'm sorry for what I've done, for what I've thought, for what I've said, for what I haven't done and said."

*Listening.* This can involve praying with Scripture.

And *praise.*

What is the difference between praise and thanksgiving? Thanksgiving is thanking God for what he's done. Praising God is praising him for who he is. They flow in and out of each other.

When it comes to God, praise can seem difficult. Yet think of what excites or interests you—maybe it's sports or music or a particular movie. If you're going to a game or a concert, you get there early. You prepare for it, and you stay until the end. And that seems right, because you're in an environment with people who enjoy the same thing. All of a sudden, however, when you show that excitement about your faith, some people think, "Well, you're going a little overboard." Really?

So praise seems the hardest part of prayer. And that brings us to a timely papal homily by Pope Francis.

## David Dancing before the Ark

The Holy Father was preaching at a daily Mass on a text from 2 Samuel 6. The ark of the covenant is making its way to Jerusalem. If you've seen the movie *The Raiders of the Lost Ark*, you'll know that the ark of the covenant is the golden box with the poles around it, inside of which is the Ten Commandments, the manna, and Aaron's rod. Everyone in Jerusalem has been anxiously awaiting it.

> And David arose and went with all the people who were with him . . . to bring up from there the ark of God. . . . And David and all the house of Israel were making merry before the LORD with all their might, with songs and lyres and harps and tambourines and castanets and cymbals. . . . And David danced before the LORD with all his might; and David was belted with a linen ephod. So David and all the house of Israel brought up the ark of the LORD with shouting, and with the sound of the horn. (2 Samuel 6:2, 5, 14-15)

Let the text give you a vision of what this looked like. This is not subdued; this is an extraordinary celebration.

> As the ark of the LORD came into the city of David, Michal the daughter of Saul [who was David's wife] looked out of the window, and saw King David leaping and dancing before the LORD; and she despised him in her heart. (2 Samuel 6:16)

We can hear her thinking, "How beneath you! How emotionally carried away you have become! Isn't this a bit too much?"

Michal the daughter of Saul came out to meet David, and said, "How the king of Israel honored himself today, uncovering himself today before the eyes of his servants' maids, as one of the vulgar fellows shamelessly uncovers himself!" (2 Samuel 6:20)

David is not naked; he is not in his underwear. A linen ephod was the clothing worn by a priest. Why is Michal upset? Because David has taken off all his kingly garments. He has divested himself of the royalty that is his. He is clothed like a priest who cares for the things of the Lord and is in reckless abandon in gratitude and praise before God. And she can't stand it.

And David said to Michal, "It was before the LORD . . .—and I will make merry before [him]." (2 Samuel 6:21)

Pope Francis reminds us that David was moved "beyond all composure." This was precisely a prayer of praise. And then he anticipates our objections:

"But, Father! This is for the Renewal in the Spirit folks, not for all Christians!" No: prayer of praise is a Christian prayer, for all of us. In the Mass, every day, when we sing the Holy, Holy, Holy . . . This is a prayer of praise: we praise God for his greatness, because he is great. We say beautiful things to him, because we are happy for his greatness "But, Father! I am not able . . . Well, you're able to shout when your team scores a goal, and you are not able to sing praises to the Lord? To come out of your shell ever so slightly to sing [his praise]? Praising God is completely gratis. [In it] we do not ask [him to give us anything]: we do not express gratitude for anything [he has given]; we praise [him]!

The Bible says that Michal ended up sterile for the rest of her life. "Those who are closed in the formality of a prayer that is cold, stingy, might end up as Michal in the sterility of her formality," Pope Francis warned. Urging us to pray "whole-heartedly," he observed, "it is also an act of justice, because he is great! He is our God." David "was so happy, because the ark was returning, the Lord was returning: his body, too, prayed with that dance."[27]

One morning five or six years ago, I was praying in our chapel on a Sunday morning, and I felt as if the Lord was speaking to me, saying, "Where is my praise? Where is the adoration that I'm due?" And the image he gave me was of something like a national championship football game when my team has the ball on their own one-yard line and they run it ninety-nine yards, all the way to the end zone. It's the single greatest play in the history of college football. It's shown over and over again.

Now compare that with this: Jesus rose from the dead. Jesus rose from the *dead*. Satan jumped on top of Jesus' back, and Satan lost. Hell jumped on top of Jesus' back, and hell lost. Death jumped on top of Jesus' back, and death lost. Where is his glory? Where is his adoration? Where is his thanksgiving? This is an act of *justice*.

People often think, "What kind of God is this who wants us to sit around and grovel in front of him by praising him?" That misses the point. It's not because he wants it; it's because we need to give it to someone. In fact, we're all giving it to someone. And the question is this: are they deserving of it? Because God is.

God became a man and took all of our sins upon himself. He went to the cross, poured out his blood, purchased our forgiveness, rose from the dead, invited us to share in his own life forever, and gave us the grace to live a great life here and now. How do we not praise him with everything we have? The Lord has won it all for you and for me. We can't go overboard or over the top.

## Praise in the Old Testament

The Scriptures confirm what Pope Francis is saying. Let's put on a biblical vision right now to look at the question of praise or worship. See if it doesn't become exceptionally clear what Scripture says to us about how we should be living.

> Rejoice in the LORD, O you righteous.
>> Praise befits the upright.
> Praise the Lord with the lyre;
>> make melody to him with the harp of ten strings!
> Sing to him a new song,
>> play skillfully on the strings, with loud shouts. (Psalm 33:1-3)

> I will bless the LORD at all times;
>> his praise shall continually be in my mouth.
> My soul makes its boast in the LORD;
>> let the humble hear and be glad.
> O magnify the LORD with me,
>> and let us exalt his name together! (Psalm 34:1-3)

Clap your hands, all peoples!
Shout to God with loud songs of joy!
For the LORD, the Most High, is awesome,
a great king over all the earth.
He subdued peoples under us,
and nations under our feet. (Psalm 47:1-3)

How *awesome* is our God! One priest in our archdiocese once said that if we saw God right now, we would explode, because he is so beautiful. We recognize beauty when we see it. We might be captivated by a sunset or the northern lights or an attractive person. But when our eyes someday behold God face-to-face in the beatific vision, then we will know what true beauty looks like.

Let the peoples praise you, O God;
let all the peoples praise you!
Let the nations be glad and sing for joy,
for you judge the peoples with equity
and guide the nations upon earth. (Psalm 67:3-4)

It is good to give thanks to the LORD,
to sing praises to your name, O Most High;
to declare your merciful love in the morning,
and your faithfulness by night,
to the music of the lute and the harp,
to the melody of the lyre.
For you, O LORD, have made me glad by your work;
at the works of your hands I sing for joy. (Psalm 92:1-4)

What are God's works? I'm alive! I'm alive, and I am forgiven, and God calls me his friend. The ground hasn't opened up and swallowed me, despite all my sins. God doesn't just tolerate me; he loves me! So I respond by praising God.

In fact, it's not just human beings who are to praise the Lord. All of creation is entering into this song of praise.

> Let the sea roar, and all that fills it;
>> the world and those who dwell in it!
> Let the floods clap their hands;
>> let the hills sing for joy together
> before the LORD, for he comes
>> to judge the earth. (Psalm 98:7-9)

> Mountains and all hills,
>> fruit trees and all cedars!
> Beasts and all cattle,
>> creeping things and flying birds!
> Kings of the earth and all peoples,
>> princes and all rulers of the earth!
> Young men and maidens together,
>> old men and children!
> Let them praise the name of the LORD,
>> for his name alone is exalted;
> his glory is above earth and heaven.
> He has raised up a horn for his people,
>> praise for all his saints,
>> for the people of Israel who are near to him.
> Praise the LORD! (Psalm 148:9-14)

The Book of Psalms ends with this hymn of praise:

Praise the LORD!
Praise God in his sanctuary;
   praise him in his mighty firmament!
Praise him for his mighty deeds;
   praise him according to his exceeding greatness!
Praise him with trumpet sound;
   praise him with lute and harp!
Praise him with timbrel and dance;
   praise him with strings and pipe!
Praise him with sounding cymbals;
   praise him with loud clashing cymbals!
Let everything that breathes praise the LORD!
Praise the Lord!" (Psalm 150:1-6)

Here are some other psalms of praise: Psalms 66, 95, 98, 147, and 149. Also, take a look at the Book of Daniel, chapter 3, for a long litany of the three men, Shadrach, Meshach, and Abednego, who sing of God's praises while in the fiery furnace.

Before we focus on the Book of Revelation, I want to point out two other passages. Colossians 3:16 says, "Let the word of Christ dwell in you richly, as you teach and admonish one another in all wisdom, and as you sing psalms and hymns and spiritual songs with thankfulness in your hearts to God." And in Ephesians 5:18-20, St. Paul writes, "Be filled with the Spirit, addressing one another in psalms and hymns and spiritual songs, singing and making melody to the Lord with all your heart, always and for everything giving thanks in the name of our Lord Jesus Christ to God the Father."

This is supposed to be part of the Christian life! We gather together and we worship. Not simply in formal places, but also informally. This is the Christian community—*alive!*

## The Worship in Heaven

Let's look at several passages from Revelation to see what is happening in heaven, mindful that we want to try to live the life of heaven now. To understand Revelation, you have to understand that it is a liturgical book; there are descriptions of incense, an altar, and vestments. Everything happens on the "Lord's Day," which is Sunday. This is John's vision:

> After this I looked, and behold, in heaven an open door! And the first voice, which I had heard speaking to me like a trumpet, said, "Come up here." . . . At once I was in the Spirit, and behold, a throne stood in heaven, with one seated on the throne! And he who sat there appeared like jasper and carnelian . . . (Revelation 4:1, 2-3)

Jasper and carnelian are precious and semiprecious stones. Notice that over and over again, John uses the word "like"—it was "like" this because John is trying to describe the indescribable.

> . . . and round the throne was a rainbow that looked like an emerald. Round the throne were twenty-four thrones, and seated on the thrones were twenty-four elders, clothed in white garments, with golden crowns upon their heads. From the throne issue flashes of lightning, and voices and peals of thunder, and before the throne . . . there is as it were a sea of glass like crystal.

And round the throne, on each side of the throne, are four living creatures, . . . and day and night they never cease to sing, / "Holy, holy, holy, is the Lord God Almighty, who was and is and is to come!"

And whenever the living creatures give glory and honor and thanks to him who is seated on the throne, who lives for ever and ever, the twenty–four elders fall down before him who is seated on the throne and worship him who lives for ever and ever; they cast their crowns before the throne, singing, / "Worthy are you, our Lord and God, / to receive glory and honor and power, / for you created all things, / and by your will they existed and were created." (Revelation 4:3-5, 6, 8-11)

Imagine something like the Oscars. Everyone is getting excited to see all these beautiful people getting out of their cars and walking down the red carpet. We say, "Oh, look how beautiful he or she is!" There is something in us that sees beauty, and we respond. Revelation is trying to help us understand that the beauty we see here on earth is nothing compared to the beauty that awaits us in heaven.

And when he had taken the scroll, the four living creatures and the twenty-four elders fell down before the Lamb, each holding a harp, and with golden bowls full of incense, which are the prayers of the saints; and they sang a new song, saying, / "Worthy are you to take the scroll and to open its seals, / for you were slain and by your blood you ransomed men for God / from every tribe and tongue and people and nation, / and have made them a kingdom and priests to our God, / and they shall reign on earth." (Revelation: 5:8-10)

This is why Jesus is so deserving of our praise: he was slain, and by his blood he has ransomed us. And he didn't do this for just a few of us; he did it for the whole world.

> I looked, and behold, a great multitude which no man could number, from every nation, from all tribes and peoples and tongues, standing before the throne and before the Lamb, clothed in white robes, with palm branches in their hands, and crying out with a loud voice, "Salvation belongs to our God who sits upon the throne, and to the Lamb!" And all the angels stood round the throne and round the elders and the four living creatures, and they fell on their faces before the throne and worshiped God, saying, "Amen! Blessing and glory and wisdom and thanksgiving and honor and power and might be to our God for ever and ever! Amen." . . .
>
> Then the seventh angel blew his trumpet, and there were loud voices in heaven, saying, "The kingdom of the world has become the kingdom of our Lord and of his Christ, and he shall reign for ever and ever." (Revelation 7:9-12; 11:15)

This is it! Fear, war, suffering, sickness, death—all have ended, and heaven descends to earth. This is the extraordinary culmination of history, and we enter into the life of heaven.

> And the twenty-four elders who sit on their thrones before God fell on their faces and worshiped God, saying, / "We give thanks to you, Lord God Almighty, who are and who were, / that you have taken your great power and begun to reign. / The nations raged, but your wrath came, / and the time for the dead to be judged, / for rewarding your servants, the prophets and saints, /

and those who fear your name, both small and great, / and for destroying the destroyers of the earth." (Revelation 11:16-18)

Here is the last passage I want to share with you, from Revelation 19:

After this I heard what seemed to be the mighty voice of a great multitude in heaven, crying, / "Hallelujah! Salvation and glory and power belong to our God, / for his judgments are true and just; / he has judged the great harlot who corrupted the earth with her fornication, / and he has avenged on her the blood of his servants."

Once more they cried, / "Hallelujah!" . . . / And the twenty-four elders and the four living creatures fell down and worshiped God who is seated on the throne, saying, "Amen. Hallelujah!" And from the throne came a voice crying, / "Praise our God, all you his servants, / you who fear him, small and great."

Then I heard what seemed to be the voice of a great multitude, like the sound of many waters and like the sound of mighty thunderpeals, crying, / "Hallelujah! For the Lord our God the Almighty reigns. / Let us rejoice and exult and give him the glory, / for the marriage of the Lamb has come, / and his Bride has made herself ready." (19:1-3, 4-7)

Note the marriage between Christ and his bride, the Church. There is a marriage in the beginning of Scripture, which is Adam and Eve's, and there is a marriage at the middle of Scripture, which is God's wedding of humanity in the person of Jesus, and now there is a marriage at the end of Scripture, when the Church comes home.

## Our Prayer in the Liturgy

As I said, the Book of Revelation is about liturgy. The Mass is liturgy, so we cannot dance in our pews on Sunday—we kneel or stand because the whole congregation is doing these things together. Yet when we are following the same rituals week after week, how do we stay engaged?

Some people find it helpful to follow the Mass in a devotional or missal. Some people find closing their eyes to be helpful so that they are not distracted. One of the most practical things you can do to avoid being a silent spectator is to come to Mass early. We go early to a football game. If we come late to a concert or play, we can't be seated until there is a pause or intermission. But because for so many of us, the Mass is "the same thing every Sunday," somehow we come with no expectations.

The danger for us who are Catholic—and not just for us who are Catholic but for us who are human—is that it is easy for everything to become rote. You can try all you want to escape from ritual, but you can't. To be human is to ritualize everything. It's what we do. That's why going to someone else's home for Thanksgiving is awkward because we don't know what they do. We all have our own habits and customs. And we do that in prayer. We want to be careful that we don't get trapped in cold, formal prayer where everything becomes rote.

We can "sleepwalk" through the Mass. When we hear, "through Christ our Lord," whether it's at the end of a prayer or not, we can be like Pavlov's dog and respond, "Amen," without ever thinking about it. This can happen whether you are ordained or not—and it's a challenge.

Here are three helpful quotes from Vatican II's *Sacrosanctum Concilium* (The Constitution on the Sacred Liturgy):

> But in order that the liturgy may be able to produce its full effects, it is necessary that the faithful come to it with proper dispositions, that their minds should be attuned to their voices, and that they should cooperate with divine grace lest they receive it in vain (cf. 2 Corinthians 6:1). Pastors of souls must therefore realize that, when the liturgy is celebrated, something more is required than the mere observation of the laws governing valid and licit celebration; it is their duty also to ensure that the faithful take part fully aware of what they are doing, actively engaged in the rite, and enriched by its effects. (11)

It's great that what we do, we do according to the rubrics. But our hearts need to be involved.

> Mother Church earnestly desires that all the faithful should be led to that full, conscious, and active participation in liturgical celebrations which is demanded by the very nature of the liturgy. (14)

Somehow the phrase "full, conscious, and active" has come to mean, "Well, you need to be a lector" or "You need to be an extraordinary minister" or "You should be an usher." That's not what it means—it doesn't have anything to do with whether or not we are performing a role in the liturgy. But when we are sitting in our pew, we want to be fully and actively and consciously engaged. Otherwise, we're just going through the motions.

Continuing with paragraph 14,

In the restoration and promotion of the sacred liturgy, this full and active participation by all the people is *the aim* to be considered before all else. (emphasis added).

And here's this last quote, which I think is the most powerful:

The Church, therefore, earnestly desires that Christ's faithful, when present at this mystery of faith, should not be there as strangers or silent spectators; on the contrary, through a good understanding of the rites and prayers they should take part in the sacred action *conscious of what they are doing,* with devotion and full collaboration. (48, emphasis added)

In other words, when you come to Mass, you are not watching me say Mass. It's *our* prayer. We just have different parts. And whom do you, as the person in the pew, collaborate with? With the Lord and with the priest, all working together to bring to God our offering. It's our prayer, our praise, and our thanksgiving.

As we have looked through Scripture, I hope it's become evident to you that as disciples and would-be saints, we are supposed to praise the Lord. We may have different temperaments—we don't all have to become charismatics—but it is right and just for us to praise God. It is an act of justice.

## QUESTIONS FOR REFLECTION AND DISCUSSION

1. This is taken from Pope Francis' homily: "How am I doing vis á vis a prayer of praise?" Do you know how to praise the Lord? If not, why not?

2. Do you know how to praise the Lord when you come to Mass? Is your whole heart really in it, or do you merely mouth the words? What have you found helpful to avoid being a "silent spectator"?

3. What does David's dancing say to you? (His wife thought it was inappropriate, but she was rebuked.)

4. Have you ever attended a praise and worship night? If not, after soaking in these Scriptures, would you ever consider going to one?

## Chapter 8

# The Primacy of Love

When we talk about becoming holy, what do we often think? After all, this is the Omega—our sanctification, as St. Paul says in 1 Thessalonians 4:3. When we think about holiness, perhaps we think about the saints, or about being pure and perfect and full of God's grace.

But that's problematic. Because, as Pope Francis has emphasized, holiness is not the accumulation of virtues. Holiness is being possessed by God.

There is a danger in the Church, as well as in our own lives, to think that holiness is about us acquiring a whole set of habits of self-control and self-discipline. We focus on how we control our time, how we spend our money, what we do with our bodies, and so forth. Yet if we're not careful, this way of looking at holiness can become a very isolated, individualistic, and dangerous way to live.

I say dangerous because such a mind-set doesn't look *out*. It somehow misses the other. For example, people commonly ask me, "Father, my cousin is getting married in a park. They are Catholic, and I know they shouldn't get married in a park. Can I go?" Now, I don't want to oversimplify a problem like that, but almost always what is behind the question is not so much a love for the person but a fear that I might somehow get a spiritual disease, if you will, by going to such a wedding— that I would be "infected," and that it would erode my own holiness. What we should be doing is asking the Lord, "Jesus, what should I do so as to win over this person?" Sometimes the answer might be "Don't go," and sometimes the answer might be "Go." The point is not so much the answer as how we begin to approach the question, whatever the question might be. When we focus only on the accumulation of virtues, we stop focusing on the real end of holiness, which is love.

Who is God? Scripture says that God is love (1 John 4:8). That is really important: God *is* love. Therefore, to be possessed by him *has* to mean that you and I look more like him. And if God is love, and to be possessed by him is to look more like him, we have to love. The Omega, our sanctification, is love.

Love isn't sappy. The challenge is to remember that love doesn't mean being "nice." "Nice" comes from a Latin word that means ignorant. Jesus was not *nice*. "Nice" is not a virtue; kindness is a virtue. So when we talk about love, we're not talking about being nice. We are talking about looking more and more like God. That's what it means to be a saint.

In this chapter, I want to discuss what it means to love, to be a saint, in the context of a Christian community, and specifically in a parish. How do we love, how do we reach out to others, as members of a parish? First, I want to focus on what a parish is—a collection of exiles—and what it should be, a place of safety for those who are lost. Then I want to talk about our need to be accountable in our walk with the Lord and the primacy of love in all that we do in our lives and in our parishes. Finally, I'll discuss the need for us, who are striving for sainthood, to move from being a consumer to a servant in our Christian communities and parishes.

## On a Journey Together

The word for "parish" in Greek is *paroikia*, which comes from the word for "exile," meaning "stranger," "sojourner," "alien." To be a parish is to be a collection of exiles. That means that this is not our home. We are walking together as brothers and sisters, trying to encourage and exhort one another, support one another, love one another, and help one another get *home*.

As a collection of exiles, we meet at a specific time and place around an altar and are nourished by the food that is the fulfillment of the food that the Israelites received when they were on their way to the Promised Land. God brought the Israelites out of slavery in Egypt and fed them in the desert with manna. Once they got to the Promised Land, there was no more manna. As we walk through our sojourn, our wanderings through the desert, the Lord takes care of us, giving us supernatural food. Once we get home, there will be no more Eucharist. Everything the Eucharist points to, you and I will experience in a completely different way in heaven. Our lives will change entirely.

Let's look at a passage from the early part of the Acts of the Apostles through this lens of being an exile. Luke is describing the early Christian community, and he makes it a point to talk about how many people sold all their possessions and put the money at the feet of the apostles so as to distribute it to the poor (Acts 2:44-45). Why would he make a big deal about that? Because it's not true that he who dies with the most toys wins. Instead, he who dies with the most toys just dies and is judged by what he did with those toys. Once we come to understand that, then all of a sudden we have tremendous freedom with the stuff that God has put at our disposal. We are free to love; we no longer have to worry about our possessions or obtaining everything here.

We can look at this idea of being an exile when we think of death as well. We grieve deeply and intensely over the loss of our family members, our children, our spouses, our parents, our friends. Yet when I lose someone I love, while I grieve deeply, I know that I will see that person again. That's because there is a home, and we're headed there, and it's very real.

## A City on a Hill

Jesus said, "You are the light of the world. A city set on a hill cannot be hidden" (Matthew 5:14). My second point is this: every Christian is supposed to be a city on a hill, and every Christian community is supposed to be a city on a hill. Why do you build a city on a hill? Not so you can see it but so that you can protect it. Have you ever been in Italy? As you drive through the countryside of Tuscany, you see all these towns built on top of mountains. They were built there for protection.

But why do you light up that city? You light it up so that people who are lost in the wilderness will see it and know where they can find safety. That's what parishes are supposed to be—places where people know they can find safety. What does that mean? It means that people will encounter the love of God and be treated with respect and dignity. It means they will find warmth and friendship and be welcomed. People will notice them and say, "I don't think I've seen you here before. Are you new? Can I help you?" It isn't just the task of the priest to reach out and bring people to our parishes;

it's everyone's task. The essence of being Christian is to be missionary.

Just the other day, someone was telling me about a discussion among some folks in his small group. They were talking about how members of the non-Catholic churches so often invite others to come to their churches. "Frankie, you should come to church on Tuesday" or "Frankie, you should come to church on Wednesday" or "Frankie, you should come to church on Thursday." One of the members of the small group remarked, "Shouldn't we be doing that as well?" And the other person said, "We don't do *that*." We don't? We don't invite people to church? We don't invite the lost to encounter Jesus? Why not?

Remember the words of Pope Francis: "The primary reason for evangelizing is the love of Jesus which we have received, the experience of salvation which urges us to ever greater love of him. What kind of love would not feel the need to speak of the beloved, to point him out, to make him known?" (*Evangelii Gaudium,* 264). Is this true for you and me?

If it's really true that having encountered Jesus is, hands down, the *best* thing that's ever happened in my life, why do I not tell someone else? If I'm convinced that knowing him, not following a bunch of rules, not living a new ethical way of life, but *knowing* him, is the best gift that anyone can receive, how am I not eager to share it?

I know that for many of us, this whole idea of being an evangelizing parish is foreign. But as we look at the Scriptures, we recognize that the early Christians lived this way. That's how Christians have always lived, so maybe we are the ones who are missing something.

We *do* do that. Because remember, we didn't build a city and then put walls around it to keep people out. We're not a ghetto. We don't keep people out; we bring people in. We should be eager to tell everyone we know about the One whom we meet here. A parish is supposed to be a place of safety for those who are lost. And goodness knows, we are surrounded by countless people who are lost.

When we extend an invitation to someone to come to church, should we invite them to Mass? Since the prayers and rituals at Mass can seem confusing to someone who wasn't raised Catholic and since that person can't receive Communion, sometimes it's better to begin by inviting someone to a program like Alpha or to a Bible study. Ultimately, of course, we want to bring that person to the "source and summit" of our lives, which is the Eucharist (*Catechism*, 1324). But we do invite people. We *do* do that.

## Mature Discipleship

My third point is this: you and I have to be mature disciples. That means that we have to be accountable and take responsibility for our walk with Jesus. We have to take the initiative. For so long, we've looked to Sister or to Father to somehow inspire us, and there's nothing wrong with that. I love helping people find the Lord; that's why I gave my life to God.

But sometimes the questions we ask the clergy or religious wouldn't be necessary if, in fact, we had some important things in place, like a habit of prayer or of reading Scripture or of getting together regularly with a group of people who also want to grow in discipleship.

You have to take responsibility for your walk with Jesus. No one else, especially not your parish priest, can make a plan for you to become a disciple and saint. No one else knows what is going on inside your heart; only you do. If we're serious about this, it demands that we sit down and say to God, "Lord, help me put my life together." Now, a priest might need to sit down with you initially to give you a couple of ideas and ask you, "How does that sound to you?" But then you have to do the work.

Have you ever wondered about the really strange parable of the wise and foolish virgins in Matthew 25? Sometimes Jesus says things that are just hard to understand; maybe for you this parable is one of them.

"'Then the kingdom of heaven shall be compared to ten maidens who took their lamps and went to meet the bridegroom. Five of them were foolish, and five were wise. For when the foolish took their lamps, they took no oil with them; but the wise took flasks of oil with their lamps. As the bridegroom was delayed, they all slumbered and slept. But at midnight there was a cry, 'Behold, the bridegroom! Come out to meet him.' Then all those maidens rose and trimmed their lamps. And the foolish said to the wise, 'Give us some of your oil, for our lamps are going out.' But the wise replied, 'Perhaps there will not be enough for us and for you; go rather to the dealers and buy for yourselves.' And while they went to buy, the bridegroom came, and those who were ready went in with him to the marriage feast; and the door was shut. Afterward the other maidens came also, saying, 'Lord, lord, open to us.' But he replied, 'Truly, I say to you, I do not know you.' Watch therefore, for you know neither the day nor the hour." (Matthew 25:1-13)

What is the point of that? Here are ten virgins; five of them bring preparations and five of them don't, for whatever reason. When the oil runs out, the first group of virgins asks the others, "Can we have some of your oil?" And they reply, "NO!" And Jesus says, "Be like them!"

Let's try to understand this. What is the oil? The oil is friendship with Jesus. And you can't give me *your* friendship with Jesus. You can't give me *a* friendship with Jesus; I'm the only one who can respond to Jesus. The Lord shows up in this parable, and the five foolish virgins realize, "We don't have a relationship with you." Then they try to get one, because all of a sudden, it's clear to them who the Bridegroom is. But it's too late.

So we need to encourage one another. We could say to one another, "Join a Bible study" or "Go to Eucharistic adoration" or "Find a small group of people to support you." These are the things that can change our lives by helping us develop a friendship with Jesus. If we are not doing these things, we need to make the time for them. Because for most of us, the reality is not "I don't have the time" but "I'm not making the time."

So where do you start? The season of Lent is an extraordinary time to begin working on a plan to grow in holiness. So often during Lent, people choose to give up chocolate or alcohol or to lose weight. But whether or not we make it to the end of Lent without taking a drink is not the point. The goal of Lent is to grow in holiness, not in self-discipline for the sake of self-discipline. So whether Lent is coming up soon or not, make a plan that will help you grow so that you will look more like Jesus.

As you think about what it is that you need to be accountable for, don't get overly ambitious. Don't say, "I'm going to do all these things: I'm going to pray an hour a day, I'm going to read a whole letter in the Scriptures every day, I'm going to fast, and I'm going to tithe." Just pick one. Ask yourself, "What is the one thing in my life right now that is most obstructing me from growing in holiness and really loving God and others as I should?"

## "The Greatest of These Is Love"

That brings me to my fourth point: the primacy of love. As St. Paul wrote, "Faith, hope, love abide, these three; but the greatest of these is love" (1 Corinthians 13:13). We will go back to 1 Corinthians 13, but let's first look at a few other passages.

First, "Let love be sincere" (Romans 12:9, NABRE). I love that word "sincere." In Latin it means "without wax." Imagine yourself as a first-century Roman shopping for a statue. The cheap statues are all made out of wax while the mid-priced ones are a combination of marble and wax. But the top-of-the-line statues are *sinceris*—all marble and no wax. That's what Paul is saying. Let your love be genuine and authentic, nothing fake or insincere.

Paul continues, "Hate what is evil, hold fast to what is good; love one another with brotherly affection; outdo one another in showing honor" (Romans 12:9-10). God has made us in such a way that we want to be honored. That's not a sin; that's how he's made us. I long to have approval. But ultimately, the approval we desire is from the Lord. We want to hear him say to us, "Well done, good and faithful servant" (Matthew 25:23).

In his essay *The Weight of Glory*, C. S. Lewis wrote, "To please God . . . to be a real ingredient in the divine happiness . . . —it seems impossible, a weight or burden of glory which our thoughts can hardly sustain. But so it is."[28] That's what we're living for. Because we're either going to hear "Well done; I am so pleased with you" or "Depart from me" (Matthew 7:23), which none of us want to hear.

There is nothing wrong with longing for our Father's approval. The problem is that we often do things longing for human approval. That can make life very problematic. If I'm doing what I'm doing so that someone will come up to me repeatedly and say, "You're a great guy; you're doing a wonderful job," then I'm in the wrong line of work. If we volunteer in church, if we help out in a ministry, and we're doing it so as to be recognized, we should stop doing it.

Having said that, we also need to be on the lookout for opportunities to honor others, which is a way to show love. "Outdo one another in showing honor," Paul says. We should be mindful of what other people do and then say, "Thank you." We should also ask for forgiveness when we take for granted the things that people do for others and for ourselves.

Let's look at what Paul says in this passage:

> But in the following instructions I do not commend you, because when you come together it is not for the better but for the worse. For, in the first place, when you assemble as a Church, I hear that there are divisions among you; and I partly believe it, for there must be factions among you in order that those who are genuine among you may be recognized. (1 Corinthians 11:17-19)

How many of us do certain things that are above and beyond what the Church requires, especially liturgically, but we're afraid to give them up? Maybe we think they are pious practices, and they might, in fact, be pious practices, but unfortunately, they often cause divisions within the churches. For example, we can make judgments about fellow parishioners just because they take Communion in their hands instead of on their tongues.

Here is the killer line; this is how Paul follows up on his observation that there are factions among the community when they assemble together: "When you meet together, it is not the Lord's supper that you eat" (1 Corinthians 11:20). What an indictment! This is Paul writing to a Christian church in Corinth that regularly gathers to celebrate Mass. But because of the division in the community, because of the lack of love among them, it's not Mass they are celebrating when they come together.

Here is a passage that we often cite when we talk about the importance of being free of deadly sin when we receive the Eucharist: "Whoever, therefore, eats the bread or drinks the cup of the Lord in an unworthy manner will be guilty of profaning the body and blood of the Lord" (1 Corinthians 11:27). That's one of the reasons why we talk about needing to be in a state of grace when we go to Communion.

But look at the next two verses: "Let a man examine himself, and so eat of the bread and drink of the cup. For any one who eats and drinks without *discerning the body* eats and drinks judgment upon himself" (1 Corinthians 11:28-29, emphasis added). Here Paul is referring not just to Christ's body in the Eucharist but to the body of Christ, the Church.

Our hearts have to love like Jesus when we walk into church and walk out again. We can't be thinking negative thoughts about other people or talking about other people when Mass is over. If we don't love the body of Christ as Christ, it doesn't matter if we looked really pious or said all the right words.

## We Are One Body

We often hear 1 Corinthians 13 at weddings, but it doesn't have anything to do with marriage specifically—it's about the community. It's about what is going on in the body of Christ. Paul is talking about all the different gifts that are present in the body of Christ, and then he says that if we really want the best gift, we need to strive for love.

> If I speak in the tongues of men and of angels, but have not love, I am a noisy gong or a clanging cymbal. And if I have prophetic powers, and understand all mysteries and all knowledge, and if I have all faith, so as to remove mountains, but have not love, I am nothing. If I give away all I have, and if I deliver my body to be burned, but have not love, I gain nothing.
>
> Love is patient and kind; love is not jealous or boastful; it is not arrogant or rude. Love does not insist on its own way; it is not irritable or resentful; it does not rejoice at wrong, but rejoices in the right. Love bears all things, believes all things, hopes all things, endures all things. (1 Corinthians 13:1-7)

I can be so eloquent, I can read your soul, I can be generous to a fault, I give away everything I have or tithe generously, but if I don't have love, I've gained nothing.

Here is something you can do: take this passage and substitute your name for the word "love." (When I do that, I stop at the first line: "Love is patient; love is kind"!) But this can help us to see if these statements apply to us, and what it is that needs the most work in us.

Let's look at several passages from St. Paul's Letter to the Ephesians.

> I therefore, a prisoner for the Lord, beg you to walk in a manner worthy of the calling to which you have been called, with all lowliness and meekness, with patience, forbearing one another in love, eager to maintain the unity of the Spirit in the bond of peace. (Ephesians 4:1-3)

Meekness doesn't mean being a quiet and timid church mouse. "Meekness" is the word that is used to describe how to break a horse. It means "strength under control." That is who Jesus is; he is meek. He is the pure power of God, always under control. Everything he does, he does out of love.

> Put off the old man that belongs to your former manner of life and is corrupt through deceitful lusts, and be renewed in the spirit of your minds, and put on the new man, created after the likeness of God in true righteousness and holiness. Therefore, putting away falsehood, let every one speak the truth with his neighbor, for we are members one of another. (Ephesians 4:22-25)

We are *one* body. It's not an image; it's a reality. We are *one* body. When one member hurts, we all hurt.

Be angry but do not sin; do not let the sun go down on your anger, and give no opportunity to the devil. (Ephesians 4:26-27)

Let no evil talk come out of your mouths, but only such as is good for edifying, as fits the occasion, that it may impart grace to those who hear. And do not grieve the Holy Spirit of God, in whom you were sealed for the day of redemption. Let all bitterness and wrath and anger and clamor and slander be put away from you, with all malice, and be kind to one another, tenderhearted, forgiving one another, as God in Christ forgave you. (Ephesians 4:29-32)

Therefore be imitators of God, as beloved children. And walk in love, as Christ loved us and gave himself up for us. (Ephesians 5:1-2)

Related to these passages from Ephesians are these verses from Colossians, chapter 3.

If then you have been raised with Christ, seek the things that are above, where Christ is, seated at the right hand of God. . . .

Put to death therefore what is earthly in you: immorality, impurity, passion, evil desire, and covetousness, which is idolatry. On account of these the wrath of God is coming. In these you once walked, when you lived in them. But now put them all away: anger, wrath, malice, slander, and foul talk from your mouth. Do not lie to one another, seeing that you have put off the old man with his practices and have put on the new man, who is being renewed in knowledge after the image of his creator. . . .

Put on then, as God's chosen ones, holy and beloved, compassion, kindness, lowliness, meekness, and patience, forbearing one another and, if one has a complaint against another, forgiving each other; as the Lord has forgiven you, so you also must forgive. And over all these put on love, which binds everything together in perfect harmony. (3:1, 5-10, 12-14)

Don't misunderstand what Paul is saying. There is no attempt here to create some idyllic community where everyone is always getting along. Some of us rub each other the wrong way—we're sandpaper against one another. You don't agree with me on a whole lot of things; I don't agree with you on a whole lot of things. So what? We are still one body.

As fallen human beings, the nature of our life together is that we are going to offend one another at times. Here's the key: at least in the body of Christ, *never presume that someone intended to offend you.* If you and I don't understand something, we should always start by saying, "I'm not sure what you meant there. I didn't catch that. What are you trying to say? What did you mean?" Instead, we often attack one another.

Remember too that online communication is even more perilous than conversation because we can't hear the tone that's intended. When it's not something cut-and-dry, when there is some emotion involved, we can easily misunderstand one another. Then we have to pick up the phone and ask, "What are you talking about?" But in the meantime, we've gotten ourselves all worked up, often for no reason.

As believers, we have to assume that if I didn't get it, either I didn't understand it or you didn't communicate as well as you should have. But we have to start with this premise: "You are my brother; you are my sister. I love you, and you love me. Let's try to figure this out." We may clash, but that's okay. We have to learn to argue in charity.

St. John is abundantly clear on the litmus test, if you will, of what it means to be a Christian. A real Christian, according to John in his letters, is a witness to and a public declaration of faith and love for the brethren.

> For this is the message which you have heard from the beginning, that we should love one another. . . . We know that we have passed out of death into life, because we love the brethren. . . . By this we know love, that he laid down his life for us; and we ought to lay down our lives for the brethren. (1 John 3:11, 14, 16)

> Beloved, let us love one another; for love is of God, and he who loves is born of God and knows God. He who does not love does not know God; for God is love. In this the love of God was made manifest among us, that God sent his only-begotten Son into the world, so that we might live through him. In this is love, not that we loved God but that he loved us and sent his Son to be the expiation for our sins. Beloved, if God so loved us, we also ought to love one another. (1 John 4:7-11)

That's a must. We *must* love one another. And just in case John is not clear enough for us, here is this verse:

> If any one says, "I love God," and hates his brother, he is a liar; for he who does not love his brother whom he has seen, cannot love God whom he has not seen. (1 John 4:20)

Jesus tells us the same thing in John 13:35: "By this all will know that you are my disciples, if you have love for one another."

## Moving from Consumer to Servant

Now for my last point: what do I mean when I say that we have to move from being a consumer to a servant? Unfortunately, many of us approach church as if we're consumers with a consumer mentality: I'm paying you for a product, and as long as you give me a decent product, I'm here. Once I don't like what you're offering me and I can find a better product elsewhere, I'm gone.

But that's not what it means to belong to a church. A church is a community. A church isn't a place where I'm simply going to get something. A church is a place where, sooner or later, I begin to ask, "What can I *give*?" And I'm not thinking about money; I'm thinking about time and talents. If we're serious about discipleship and about becoming saints, we should be asking, "How can I serve? What can I do? How can I help?" Parishes should be bursting at the seams with volunteers. That's how we love one another.

The Catherine of Siena Institute's Called and Gifted Seminar is a tremendous tool that helps people understand the charisms that God has given them so they can know what their gifts are. This enables them to come forward and say, "Father, I think the Lord has blessed me in this way. I'd like to put it in the service of the parish somehow. What can I do?"

So we want to move from being consumers who are purchasing something to being servants who realize, "This is my family. How do I take care of it?" What can we do, right now, so that our family can be more the place it's supposed to be? How can other people know that this is a place of safety? What can we do to encourage one another to take responsibility for our lives? How can we, all of us, collectively, be on the lookout for making our Christian communities places where Christian charity is *experienced*?

That's not the priest's task. That's *your* task. Pastors and priests will come and go every few years, but you will, in all likelihood, still be in that parish family. What kind of family do you want it to be?

The fire that burns in that little tabernacle in your church can become a big blaze. Your parish really can be known as a place where people encounter Jesus. It can be known as a place where people walk in and feel loved. It can be a place where the Spirit is alive and we're eager to tell others about him. But that means that all of us have to roll up our sleeves and get to work.

Wherever your parish is right now, know that the Lord wants to pour out his grace. Even if you are moving towards making, forming, and missioning disciples, the Lord has more to give. Your parish can be an amazing place; it can have a great effect on the world. Don't forget what the Lord wants to tell us: "I have more!" God always has more.

## QUESTIONS FOR REFLECTION AND DISCUSSION

1. How often do I approach someone I don't know in church and welcome that person? Whom might I invite to attend a Bible study, small group, or other program at my church?

2. What is one thing I need to do to grow in holiness and become a more mature disciple of the Lord? Who might hold me accountable in this area?

3. Substitute your name for "love" in 1 Corinthians 13:4-7. In which area do you need to grow the most? Pray and ask the Lord to fill you with the grace to love as he does.

4. What do you think your gifts or charisms are? How might you use them in your parish?

5. Spend some time in prayer. What might the Lord be telling you about making love the primary aim in your life?

# Notes

1. Raniero Cantalamessa, *The Gaze of Mercy: A Commentary on Divine and Human Mercy* (Frederick, MD: The Word Among Us Press, 2015), p. 146.

2. "Pope Francis: God Has a Loving Weakness for the Lost Sheep," Vatican Radio, November 7, 2013. Accessed at http://en.radiovaticana.va/storico/2013/11/07/pope_francis_god_has_a_loving_weakness_for_the_lost_sheep/en1-744370.

3. *Diary of Saint Maria Faustina Kowalska: Divine Mercy in My Soul* (Stockbridge, MA: Marian Press, 2007), p. 420, §1146.

4. Ibid.

5. Raniero Cantalamessa, Fourth Lenten Sermon to Papal Household, April 1, 2007. Accessed at https://zenit.org/articles/4th-lenten-sermon-of-father-cantalamessa/.

6. Samuel Noah Kramer, *The Sumerians: Their History, Culture, and Character* (Chicago: University of Chicago Press, 1963, p. 123. Accessed at http://oi.uchicago.edu/sites/oi.uchicago.edu/files/uploads/shared/docs/sumerians.pdf.

7. Erasmo Leiva-Merikakis, *Fire of Mercy, Heart of the Word, Meditations on the Gospel According to Matthew,* vol. 1 (San Francisco: Ignatius Press, 1996), pp. 363–364.

8. This excerpt from a sermon by St. Augustine (Sermo 46, 10-11: CCL 41, 536-538) is used in the Roman Catholic

Office of Readings for Friday of the 24th Week in Ordinary Time. Accessed at Crossroads Initiative, https://www.crossroadsinitiative.com/media/articles/negligent-shepherds/.

9. C. S. Lewis, *The Weight of Glory and Other Addresses* (New York: HarperCollins, 1949, 2001), p. 45.

10. Here is the full quote: "As we read of the things that were done to Jesus between his arrest at Gethsemane and his sentencing to crucifixion, we get the feeling that in some way he stood outside them. As prisoner on trial for his life he was the central figure; but he seemed not to belong to the circle in which these other men moved around him. The Sanhedrin passed him on to Pilate, Pilate to Herod, Herod back to Pilate. They mocked him and scourged him. He gives an effect of almost total passivity, furiously acted upon, hardly reacting at all. The truth is that he was the central figure, but of a wider action than his tormentors knew. For he was redeeming the whole human race, his tormentors included. He was active as no man has ever been, wholly given to the greatest thing that has been done upon earth." From Frank Sheed, *To Know Christ Jesus* (San Francisco: Ignatius Press, 1980), p. 359.

11. *Summa Theologica*, Ia, Q63, Art. 2, ad. 2.

12. Raniero Cantalamessa, trans. Marsha Daigle-Williamson, *Beatitudes: Eight Steps to Happiness* (Cincinnati: Servant Books, 2011), p. 4.

13. Ibid., p. 5.

14. Tadeusz Dajczer, *The Gift of Faith* (Fort Collins, CO: In the Arms of Mary Foundation, 2005), pp. 56–57.

15. Timothy Keller, Sermon podcast, "Everyone with a Gift," January 24, 2014. Accessed at https://itunes.apple.com/us/podcast/everyone-with-a-gift/id352660924?i=1000120028378&mt=2.

16. Ibid.

17. Ibid, emphasis added.

18. Fr. Wilfrid Stinissen, *Into Your Hands, Father: Abandoning Ourselves to the God Who Loves Us* (San Francisco: Ignatius Press, 2011), pp. 23–24. Used with permission. www.ignatius.com.

19. Ibid, pp. 9–11.

20. St. Catherine of Siena's actual quote, taken from Dialogue 66: "Now I do not want her to think about her sins individually, lest her mind be contaminated by the memory of specific ugly sins. I mean that I do not want her to, nor should she, think about her sins either in general or specifically without calling to mind the blood and the greatness of my mercy. Otherwise she will only be confounded. For if self-knowledge and the thought of sin are not seasoned with remembrance of the blood and hope for mercy, the result is bound to be confusion. And along with this comes the devil, who under the guise of contrition and hatred for sin and sorrow for her guilt leads her to eternal damnation." Quoted in *Catherine of Siena: Passion for the Truth, Compassion for Humanity* by Mary Driscoll, OP (Hyde Park, NY: New City Press, 2008), p. 96.

21. Stinissen, p. 23.

22. Ibid., p. 17.

23. Ibid., p. 49.

24. Ibid., p. 55.

25. Ibid., p. 80.

26. Ibid., p. 81.

27. "Pope Francis at Daily Mass: The Fruitfulness of Praise," January 28, 2014, Vatican Radio. Accessed at http://en.radiovaticana.va/storico/2014/01/28/pope_francis_at_daily_mass_the_fruitfulness_of_praise_/en1-768047.

28. C. S. Lewis, *The Weight of Glory and Other Addresses* (New York: HarperCollins, 1949, 2001), pp. 38–39.

# the WORD among us ®
### The Spirit of Catholic Living

This book was published by The Word Among Us. Since 1981, The Word Among Us has been answering the call of the Second Vatican Council to help Catholic laypeople encounter Christ in the Scriptures.

The name of our company comes from the prologue to the Gospel of John and reflects the vision and purpose of all of our publications: to be an instrument of the Spirit, whose desire is to manifest Jesus' presence in and to the children of God. In this way, we hope to contribute to the Church's ongoing mission of proclaiming the gospel to the world so that all people would know the love and mercy of our Lord and grow more deeply in their faith as missionary disciples.

Our monthly devotional magazine, *The Word Among Us*, features meditations on the daily and Sunday Mass readings, and currently reaches more than one million Catholics in North America and another half million Catholics in one hundred countries around the world. Our book division, The Word Among Us Press, publishes numerous books, Bible studies, and pamphlets that help Catholics grow in their faith.

To learn more about who we are and what we publish, log on to our website at www.wau.org. There you will find a variety of Catholic resources that will help you grow in your faith.

# Embrace His Word, Listen to God . . .

www.wau.org